C000000245

A tale of Subbuteo.

For Flicks
Sake!

About the Author:

Ashley Dunn is the youngest of five siblings born in Croydon, Surrey to Margaret and Victor Dunn in the early 1960's. On Christmas day 1970, aged just eight years old, he opened a Christmas present like no other from his parents. It was to spark a lifelong love affair with the greatest table-top football game ever invented: Subbuteo.

Today, Ashley is widowed and lives by the sea in Folkestone, Kent. He has two daughters and four grandchildren. Sadly, none of them are interested in playing Subbuteo.

ISBN **978-1-7399-5200-6**

Nemesis:

As defined by Cambridge Dictionaries online –

"Someone's nemesis is a person or thing that is very difficult for them to defeat".

This is my story of Subbuteo, a game I loved to play whilst growing up and the fierce rivalry that developed between two friends and work colleagues.

The story starts when I was a child, when at Christmas 1970 my parents bought me the greatest table-top football game ever invented, Subbuteo. I describe how, as a child, I found "my team" and how they became my champions, beating all-comers.

As a young adult, I go on to describe "life in the 1980's office" and the "politically incorrect" banter that was shared by all. And how an innocent discussion un-wittingly sparked a fierce rivalry with a work colleague as to who was the better player...

And they say, "It's only a game..."

For Flicks Sake!

For Dale...

And for Me.

Contents

Chapter 1.
In the beginning...

I've been a BIG fan of Subbuteo, ever since I was a little boy of eight when my parents first bought me a set for Christmas. It was 1970, a time before video games and computers but an era of good old-fashioned types of family board and table games and my parents had bought me the best game of the lot. How little they would have realised that that game would have such a big effect on my life. I was to play Subbuteo pretty much every day until about the age of sixteen when I left school and went to work.

I wasn't an only child, far from it, I was the youngest of five children. I had two brothers and two sisters but the seven and eleven year age gap between my brothers and I meant that I had to play on my own a lot. My sisters, Linda and Lorraine were closer in age but had no interest in playing 'boys' games so I had to amuse myself most of the time and what better way to lose oneself in play than by playing Subbuteo. Obviously, it was meant as a two player game but it was easy enough for me to be impartial and play as both teams.

Playing for hours at a time, for days on end during the school holidays and pretty much at every opportunity after school, I became quite adept at it. I could flick those little plastic men which would spin and twist and twirl on their bases and would beat all-comers who came to my house to play.

In addition to this, I was lucky enough to have a purpose-built 'stadium' for my Subbuteo men. My father had purchased a half-sized Churchill rollover Dining-come-Billiard table many years before I was born and as luck would have it, it was the perfect size for my Subbuteo pitch. And being a Billiard table the playing surface was perfectly flat and the green baize cloth closely matched the colour of the Subbuteo pitch. It also provided a fine 'cushion' or 'spring' under the tip of your finger as you prepared to flick the players. The 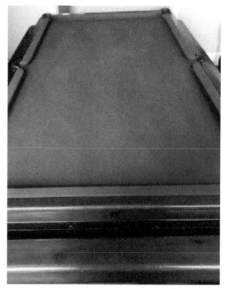 cushions of the Billiard table acted as perfect boundaries to keep the ball and the players on the table. So it had all the advantages of being a table to play the game on without the hazards most of my school friends had which was playing on their knees on the floor and the ever-present-danger of someone kneeling or standing on their players.

The set my parents had bought me was the standard, basic boxed set of Subbuteo. It had two teams, one Red, which I called Manchester United and the other Blue, which I called Leicester City or Chelsea. My brother Laurence supported Manchester United and my sister Lorraine liked Chelsea, although in truth it was Ron 'Chopper' Harris and Peter Osgood that she really liked. My dad also had the good sense to realise that you needed more than just two teams to get the full enjoyment out of this game and bought two more teams, West Ham United and Crystal Palace. My Dad and older brother Terry were West Ham supporters and me, because we lived in Croydon, supported Palace.

Now Palace in the seventies used to play in claret shirts with thin pale blue stripes which were also very similar to the West Ham team of claret shirts with pale blue sleeves. They also had the same colour bases of claret outer and pale blue inners which often caused confusion whilst playing against each other as they were not always easy to distinguish. However, my brothers and I used to make up all kinds of tournaments as we all had our own teams and in the early days, used to play an awful lot. The down-side of being the much smaller brother at the time was that my brothers got the hang of it more easily and quickly than I did at eight, so I used to lose a lot. Being bigger and taller than me they could get around the table much quicker than I and could reach further as well. I was at a real disadvantage. Also, at that age, I wasn't interested in reading the rules, I just wanted to play. So I relied on them to explain the rules to me. Unfortunately, some of the rules were quite ambiguous and led to them being mis-interpreted. This caused problems for me later on when I played my friends as the rules I was used to were not the same as what everyone else had been playing. I soon realised that the rules had not been fully read and understood by my brothers, resulting in certain 'house' rules being created. However, as it turned out the rules we played to made a lot more sense than the actual real rules by Subbuteo, so we continued to play to our rules instead. They were simpler to understand.

As I said, my brothers used to win quite regularly against me, so I practiced as often as I could and learned to flick properly and play well enough to eventually start beating them. And when I did, I realised two things; one, Laurence was quite fair and could play reasonably well and two, Terry was quite capable of inventing and bending the rules.

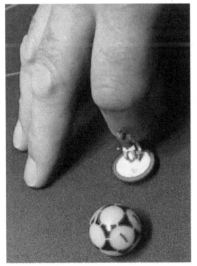

Laurence could flick the players correctly and you could have quite an enjoyable game against him as it would be played fairly and if he lost, he didn't mind. He didn't cheat. Terry, on the other hand couldn't flick properly. Well, he could, but he just wouldn't. It seems he didn't quite have the skill and dexterity we'd mastered in flicking and swerving the players to make them spin around players or the ball and as Laurence and I got better and started winning more and more games, he used a technique whereby he would drag the players with the fleshy-part of the inside of his finger. This was specifically against the rules as it was a lazy-type of flicking and there really wasn't any skill involved. You were supposed to flick the players using your finger nail. Personally, I think he was simply too lazy to move around the table to get into position to make a proper flick. He may just as well have pushed or placed his players into position. This often caused arguments as Laurence and I would object to this style of play and Terry used to argue that it was ok and that he *was* flicking, just with the *inside* of his finger. In the end, Laurence and I used to insist on one or other of us being the referee as it was the only way to get a fair game against him. Being extremely competitive, Terry could sometimes be a sore loser, which again would lead to arguments. He felt we were ganging up on him, objecting to his technique and would stomp off in a huff if

we'd blown for a foul flick. Sometimes, I didn't like to play him at all.

   There was one match, when I was about eleven, where I thrashed him Eight – Nil! Now, after all the thrashings I had received over the years, I should have enjoyed it but after the fifth goal went in and it wasn't even half-time, he couldn't be bothered to play properly and just nudged his players about the pitch. I could have easily won ten or twelve nil that day but I stopped trying in the second half as he'd spoilt the enjoyment for me. We just went through the motions and finished the game in silence. I was relieved when it ended.

Eventually though, as time wore on and with Terry and Laurence going off to work, I would be left alone with my Subbuteo set during the long school holidays and weekends. I happily played by myself, lost in my own little world of Subbuteo with no-one to disturb me. What Bliss!

So there I was, aged about nine, one school holiday when mum announced that she (which actually meant _WE_) had to go to Croydon to get some shopping. As I was so young, mum would not leave me in the house on my own and had to take me with her, which I didn't mind - except there was one place I absolutely hated going to - Surrey Street Market. I hated going there because it was always so busy and crowded, we could easily get separated and I feared I would get lost. It was a very scary place to be for a young child of eight or nine who didn't know how to find his way home if the unthinkable were ever to have happened.

Anyway, on this particular day, mum needed to go Croydon and had to take me with her. And when the weather was nice, mum would walk there and then get the bus home once she'd finished. So having warned me that we were going down Surrey Street she said that we would do that bit last and that we should not be too long. I was about to object when she said "We could stop for a look in the toy shop under the flyover, if you like...?" Even at nine years of age, I recognised bribery! That was code for "I might buy you a Subbuteo team if you come..." Instantly I was hooked.

Back in the day, *Beatties* used to be the kiddies toy shop of choice, displaying a wide variety of toys, *Airfix* models and of course the largest selection of Subbuteo and accessories I had ever seen. They had World Cup Editions, World Cup goals, Accessories, Floodlights, Trophies and Teams. One whole wall was covered with Subbuteo stuff. They had everything.

So on this warm, sunny day, mum and I walked all the way into Croydon. The walk there passed swiftly. I was eager and keen to get to Beatties and mum always walked fairly briskly. She couldn't drive and it was her way of getting a little exercise, so she always walked everywhere. We stopped at the flyover as promised and I looked in the shop window. And there, in the window staring back at me was the most amazing sight I'd ever seen! Well, in terms of Subbuteo anyway. I saw this most wonderful of looking teams. They were Red shirted, Blue shorted, White Socked, on Blue discs set on Red bases, BLACK, South American Subbuteo players. And to add additional colour, the goalie was wearing a Green shirt and together they just looked MAGNIFICENT!

Now, to put this into perspective, back in the 1970's black toy figures were few and far between. Even in professional football black players were rare. So to see a team that had *BLACK PLAYERS* was absolutely amazing. I was certain no-one I knew would have anything like it. They looked so different from any other Subbuteo team I'd ever seen. I just <u>had</u> to have them! And

there they were, waiting for me to arrive and claim them. It was fate.

Now as I said, when I was a kid I was absolutely Subbuteo mad. All-in-all I eventually amassed seventeen teams – which was a lot back then – but no one team ever had the impact on me that they did. They were – and still remain to this day – my favourites. And my mother, bless her, did what any loving mother would do for her child when saw how instantly in love with this team I was, she bought them for me.

Thank you mum.

That one simple act brought me *years* of untold pleasure.

I walked down Surrey Street market with my mum that day without a single word of complaint, clutching my little bag with my treasure trove close to my chest and with such excitement in my heart that I practically floated, such was the daze I was in. I just couldn't wait to get back home to play with them.

When we got home, I had a little ritual with all my newly purchased teams; I would get my other teams out onto the pitch and 'introduce' them to each other. Then I would randomly select one to play against the new team. Trouble was, I had no idea who this team were. There was no other team like them in England.

Later that day, when Terry got home he looked up the Subbuteo chart for me and found them. They were called *Chile*. Red and Blue coloured, and South American. I had never even heard of the place before but I loved them. From the moment I got them home and for the next few years, I played almost non-stop with them. Chile was *MY TEAM*! My next door-neighbours Stephen and Danny used to play Subbuteo (but not very well) and I used to take Chile round to their house to play and would finish the day unbeaten. At school, some of my friends also used to play Subbuteo and I would take Chile 'On tour'. I would rarely get beaten but most often would win and win convincingly. Chile were the champs, not just of my teams at home but of all of my friends and classmates alike. I cannot stress this enough; I LOVED THEM!

Even to this day, every time I open that little green box marked 'Chile' I get a thrill just looking at them.

Chile

Chapter 2.
The '80's Office.

Fast-forward a few years and I'm now a young man of twenty, working in an office in Croydon. I'm working for a large Assurance company in an open-plan office.

Back in the early 1980's the office environment was a very different place to what it is today. For instance, you were allowed to smoke at your desk and back then more people smoked than not. It seems incredible now but it was quite normal for thirty or forty people or more to be smoking in a room surrounded by hundreds and hundreds of sheets of paper. Not to mention the health risk posed to everyone in the room from the primary and secondary smoke inhalation but the potential fire hazard with all that paper, cigarettes, lighters and burning embers. It seems so bloody obvious now how dangerous it was.

Another thing, there were no desktop computers. Not even V.D.U.'s (Visual Display Units for those of you not old enough to remember them). Mainframe computers were only just starting to creep into the workplace and were big, noisy, clunking machines that needed a dedicated bunch of people to operate them. In the meantime, Assurance companies like ours were manually operated and relied upon an army of people to perform jobs that we would now take for granted with a desktop or laptop computer. For example, emails were unheard of. The writing of letters was done by the typing pool. In-coming letters were dealt with by the post room (ok, that one is still done). Tape libraries are now gone. Manual filing and microficheing are practically obsolete. Any printing would have been done on an impact line printer connected to the mainframe on perforated paper that ran on spools. All copies had to be made by the paper having sheets of carbon in-between the sheets of paper on the printer which had to be manually separated and tidied-up once it was printed. It all seems very long-winded and laborious by today's standard.

Our department was a Claims department and was made up of several teams of up to eight people per team. My team – or rather – my Team Leader's team dealt with AWP's (Automatic Withdrawal Payments) on a daily basis. The job for each of us was to separate hundreds and hundreds of sheets of paper - AWP letters - from the carbon sheets. There were three copies and each letter had to be put into separate piles, 'Client', 'File' and the 'Spare' copy which went off to be microfiched. We would then have to make a list of all the files we needed (by hand) and go to the filing room and request them. This consisted of handing our lists over to one of the two old dears who worked in there. Looking back, the room always seemed to be shrouded in smoke as both of them smoked heavily. Health and safety today would have a fit!

Finally, after waiting a couple of hours to get your requested files, the Client letters were matched-up to the corresponding cheques. They would be folded up and put into a window envelope and then periodically, old Fred from the post room would wander around the floor pushing a shopping trolley for us to chuck our letters into ready to be sent out.

All very manual and low-tech.

Letters were typed by the typing pool. If we had to write a letter, we would dictate it into a small, hand-held dictating machine and then put the tape with the relevant file and put the file on a table at the end of the section. At two-hour intervals, one of the typing-pool girls would come along and collect them.

The floor was presided over by Claims Manager, Trevor Woods or 'T-Dubs' as he was otherwise known. He was a great big, bearded, bear of a man who had the sharpest wit of anyone I've ever met in my life. Apart from being exceptionally good at his job, he was also great fun to work for. He knew exactly how to handle people and we all had the greatest respect for him.

My best-mate-at-work was a guy named Paul, or Sedge as I'd called him on account of him having bushy blonde hair. It was a cross between his surname, Seddon and hedge, so hence *Sedge*. He was a year older than me and we sat next to each other at work. We also went out socially to bars and clubs and generally had a good laugh. We had very similar interests – girls and motorbikes – and were great mates.

Sedge was the assistant team leader of our Claims section and therefore senior to me. As a result, he always joked that I had to show respect to my elders and betters i.e. him, by getting my fags out first at tea-break in the mornings.

"Dunny-boy," he would say, "I've got just one thing to say to you... Get 'em aht!" as he slurped his tea and waited for me to pass him – and light it – a Benson & Hedges cigarette.

Often, we would have a good laugh with the girls in the typing pool. One of them, Anna, a fun-loving, blond-haired, large-chested girl who had a bit of a loping walk, would come striding through our department to collect the typing files. Sedge and I would tease her by bouncing in time with her walk –

and her chest - in our chairs as she came through, making "boing, boing, boing" noises as we bounced. She always laughed and if ever we forgot to do it would call over and ask if we'd gone off her! Also, if any of the other, girls came through, Sedge and I would slap the backs of our necks in quick, Eric Morecambe-esque fashion and give a little shudder to show our 'appreciation' of a good-looking girl passing through. As the joke developed, we would often slap each other's neck.

"Quick, Dunny-boy! Quick!" Sedge would say and proffer the back of his neck for me to give it a few quick slaps. Then I'd do the same and we'd sit back and laugh and light a fag in mock relief.

Back then, political correctness had not prevented us from making such childish jokes. The girls, for their part took it all in good fun and often gave us as good back. It was well-known that Sedge, being fair haired and fair skinned would blush very easily and go very red if ever he got embarrassed. The girls used to play on this and whenever he had to go to the typing pool, he would be met by a chorus of cat-calls and wolf-whistles from the girls to embarrass the hell out of him. He used to return from there looking like a Swan Vesta matchstick! For all our bravado, we were still quite shy with the ladies.

In one of the team sections near us, there was a young man called Ray. Ray was a little bit odd but actually a very nice guy. He had a goatee beard, wore glasses and had very long thick brown hair. His hair was way past his shoulders but rather than wear it in a pony-tail or pulled back, he had it forward, like Cousin 'It' from The Munsters. This was done to cover his face. He wasn't ugly or disfigured or anything like that, he just said it was because he was painfully shy and didn't like people looking at him. But then the odd thing was he dressed rather weirdly. He wore a tweed three-piece suit, a deerstalker hat, a Sherlock Holmes tweed riding cape, had his long, wavy hair out, and smoked a large, curved, bone-handled pipe with what can only be described as large quantities of cow-dung burning out of it. How not to get noticed – Not! So hence, his nick-name was Sherlock. Actually, it got refined to No-shit-Sherlock and then reduced again to just No-shit. He took it all in good part and once you got to know him, he was a very amusing, highly intelligent guy. And funnily enough, for all his strange quirks and oddities, he was extremely popular with the girls. He was always surrounded by them, two in particular, Sharon and Jo. Sharon was one of the Team Leaders and had beautiful, straight, long brown hair. It actually reached her backside. And oh-boy, what a backside she had! Her assistant Jo, was one of the Office juniors and likewise was also very attractive. She was petite, cute, dark-haired and always bright-eyed and smiley and both girls were always with Sherlock, taking him out to lunch or for drinks after work. Jo even took his letters down to the typing pool for him, like she was his P.A. I never figured that one out until much later.

The only other person who didn't have to go to the typing pool was T-Dubs. His dictation would be collected personally by the lady in charge, Janice.

Janice was tall, slim and very good-looking. However, she hardly ever seemed to smile and rarely spoke to anyone. She had a nice figure, short, strawberry-blonde wavy hair, held her head up, shoulders back and had just an ever-so-slight wiggle in her walk which turned every head in the room. Everyone that is, except Trevor's.

T-Dubs seemed oblivious to her and only ever spoke or glanced at her when she came in to pick up his dictation. One day, after collecting his files and walking past our section, Sedge eyed her up and down, turned to T-Dubs, pulled a face and stage-whispered across the room "Cor! Trev! Wouldn't mind a bit of that eh?"

T-Dubs sniffed, nonchalantly lit a fag and said "Well, if you like that kind of thing..."

"Like that kind of... She's gorgeous mate! Especially when she wears that lilac top! Phwoar!"

Another very attractive lady on our floor was Eva. She was Polish and had a very soft, very gentle, slightly husky voice. Her full name was Eva Isobella Davé (pronounced *A-var E-so-bey-lah Dah-vey*) and although she spoke beautiful English she also had a heavy eastern European accent, which, combined with everything else, made her sound like a female vampire! She was always very well turned-out and elegantly dressed and we used to call her '*The Countess*' which she loved and would play up to it. She agreed that it was befitting of her status and breeding. All was well until one day, when old Fred from the Post Room came huffing and puffing onto our floor waving a letter in the air and shouting in his gruff '*Sarf Lunnen*' accent, "Anyone 'ere know a Missus Dave?..." Practically the whole floor fell about laughing! Poor Eva! Gone from being the aristocratic "Countess A-van-yar Dah-vey" to plain ol' "Missus Dave" in the blink of an eye. How cruel – and how funny!

The Senior Manager of the Company was a man rather pompously named Dupont. Miles

Dupont. Or, as everyone else secretly called him, 'Doopers!' If ever he was spotted walking down the corridor Sedge and I would start quietly singing "The Duke of Earl" song as an early warning signal that he was coming. Only our version was the "Doop of Earl" and sometimes all it needed was just the intro "Doop, doop, doop..." to alert everyone. However, we need not have bothered as he was his own early warning signal as he used to stomp everywhere at high speed. It was as though he were urgently trying to get somewhere or show everyone how important he was by racing around the place. He rarely ever spoke to anyone other than to his Secretary Dee or to T-Dubs. He didn't need to, T-Dubs was the floor manager and all communication went through him. Doopers would race out of his office, shout across the floor and say something like "Trevor! I need to see you in my office immediately! Dee-Dee, Come and take a letter." and stomp back to his office. Dee, the stereo-typical blonde secretary in high heels and pencil skirt would get up and as she walked past, T-Dubs would mimic Doopers and say "Yes, Dee-Dee, I want you to take something down..." and then she would reply "Yes Sir, Knickers!" and they would laugh, link arms, then go arm-in-arm stomping-off down the corridor.

It was a very happy office, even if the work could be tedious. And it was during one of those long, laborious, periods of separating pieces of paper and filling envelopes that the conversation in the department got around to our childhood and childhood toys and games we used to play with. Sedge mentioned that he liked games like Cluedo or Buckaroo. Someone else mentioned Ker-plunk, Monopoly, Operation and a few others. I stuck my head above the parapet, expecting to get ridiculed by all and sundry when I mentioned that I used to play Subbuteo... Well blow me! No sooner had I said that then a few of the others enthusiastically piped-up and said they used to play it as well. Actually, much to my surprise, one of the lads called Charlie Dodsworth owned up to *still* playing it.

Now Charlie was relatively new to the company and at twenty-two looked a little like a slightly chubby-looking Bobby Moore, the famous England football captain. He was blond, round-faced and football mad and because of his chubby build, we nick-named him *'Chubby'* or *'Chubby-Dodds'*, which seemed to suit him. Pretty much everyone there had a nick-name.

However, I must admit to saying that I never particularly liked him. There was just something underlying and nasty about him. He had quite a temper sometimes and would get very aggressive over the most trivial of things. In hindsight, he reminded me of a *'Paul Gascoigne'* (the famous footballer) type of character as he was always larking around and being stupid or irritating but he thought he was being funny. Personally, I always thought he was barking mad. For example; He supported Chelsea (there, that proves it!) but not just supporting them and being interested in their results or going to watch them like any normal fan but being *fanatically* mad about them. He knew everything about them. He could list off whole team sheets from seasons' way back and tell you how many goals a player had scored in his career and could list the whole fixture list for Chelsea for the entire season. And his favourite player at the time was a footballer called Mark Turkington. Chubby's knowledge of Football in general was encyclopaedic and probably knew more stats than the commentator, John Motson. Incidentally, he could do a very good impression of Motty as well. He also had this irritating habit of chanting football songs and shouting "Whoahhh!! It's gone innnnn!!" Or, creeping up behind you whilst you were standing at the photocopier or worse – the urinal – and shouting "Whoahhh!! What a goal!!" Or, shouting "Turkington!!" very loudly in your ear. Very bloody irritating! Especially when you were having a pee and he'd caused you to wee down your trouser leg! And if you ever bent down or leant over a desk to reach something, you really had to be on your guard because he would run up behind you and slap your backside very hard, and whilst you were jumping around in agony he would be in your face saying "Like it! Learn to love it, and ask for more!" He was mad. He also had this very odd habit of 'saluting' vintage or classic cars. He would be walking along the road with you talking about something - usually football - when out of the corner of his eye he would see an old style car. He would stand stock-still on the pavement, throw his chest out and salute, yes, *salute* the car. "Salute that car!" he would say. Then carry on as normal... very strange. But as it turned out, he was mad about Subbuteo as well. His favourite team was 'Sweden', who wore yellow shirts and blue shorts. He also said he had a stadium at home and was happy to take on all-comers. Chubby's stadium had floodlights - which I had - and a scoreboard that I also had. He also had the T.V. and Commentary tower set which I didn't have. There was one more thing which proved to me that he was barking mad and that was that he had his stereo tuned to white noise. He would stand there grinning, shouting "Turkington!" and then turn the volume up so that the white noise would sound like the roar of the crowd!

Another lad who admitted playing Subbuteo was Nigel - or *Clint* as he was known on account of his surname - Westwood - who at eighteen was the youngest of us. He had only recently joined the company and was in his first job from college. Clint was a likeable lad who had a good sense of humour about him and used to sit next to an elderly lady called Shirley, who worked on the next section. She was a lovely old dear, slightly deaf and with a soft voice and an American accent. But she also had an irritating habit of continually singing to herself or softly humming and because she was deaf, the volume of her singing would slowly rise without her realising it. Clint used to take the mickey out of her by humming *Strangers in the night* at a slightly louder volume than one would normally expect to hear someone humming but he did this to secretly draw our attention to the fact that dear old "Shirl" was at it again. However, he came unstuck one day whilst during humming *Strangers* for the third time in as many minutes when she fixed him with a cold, hard stare and said sharply "Nigel! If you must insist on humming, please do it quietly. It's irritating to me and to everyone else around you!" His slack-jawed face was a picture.

Then one day, our team leader, Alan 'Cookie' Cookson, got promoted to floor supervisor and naturally, Sedge was eyeing the vacant team leader top spot. However, it wasn't long before we got the news that Cookie's replacement had been found, recruited and had already started. The new team leader was being shown around the office by T-Dubs at that very moment. Dee-Dee, who had already met him announced rather excitedly to Sharon and Jo that the new chap was "very good-looking..." and was being introduced round the typing pool if they wanted to pop down for a sneaky look? Quick as a flash, they disappeared down the corridor. Overcome with curiosity they were swiftly followed by Sedge. A little while later he re-appeared, flushed and puffing as if he'd run all the way back.

"I've just seen our new boss!" He exclaimed. "He _is_ a good-looking bastard. All the birds in the typing pool are swooning over him."

"Oh" I said.

"Yeah, I'm gonna ditch you and be mates with him, you ugly git! That way, when the birds flock around him, I'll get his cast-offs!" he said. Then he looked at me and grinned "Not really you bald old git*, I wouldn't ditch you. Besides, you make me look good! Now get 'em aht!"

"Cheers," I thought as I fumbled for my cigarettes "can't wait to meet him."

*Note: Even though I was younger than Sedge and had only just turned twenty years old, my hair unfortunately had started to thin noticeably on top ☹

Chapter 3.
Dale.

Dale Thornley, our new manager _was_ a good-looking bastard. If George Clooney himself had walked naked through our office he would have made less of an impact than Dale did. All the women were dreamy-eyed for him. He was a little older than us at twenty-five, a shade under six feet tall, slim build, brown hair, soft brown eyes, and had a close-cropped beard. And there was something ever-so-slightly arrogant about him as he walked. He had a slight 'bounce' to his step. And one more thing; he had that all important ingredient... a _winning smile_! And he knew just how to use it with the ladies too. They just seemed to swoon at his feet or fall for his chat. It seemed effortless for him to chat to any girl he fancied. He would walk straight up to them and chat – I never did find out what his opening lines were – and he often used to come away with their phone number or had arranged to meet them for a drink later on. Very rarely did he ever get knocked-back. I've never seen anyone either before or after so successfully chat-up women. If you could have bottled it, you would have made a mint. It was amazing to watch.

However, to be fair to Dale, He was never actually big-headed about it. "It's all about confidence," he would say, "it's all in the eyes, and the smile..." Easy when you have nice eyes and a winning smile, I thought. He was also a good laugh out of work and Sedge and I often used to go out with him, drinking and clubbing with him and sometimes his best friend, Steve would come along.

Now, Dale and Steve lived in a place called Pratt's Bottom, Bexley, near Orpington, in Kent and used to drink in a local working-man's club for the cheap beer. But that wasn't the only reason they'd go there. Every Friday night they'd meet at the club, have a few beers, play darts then go off to a more fashionable bar or club to drink and partake of Dale's other favourite pastime, 'pulling'. But before they left, they would finish off at the working-man's club with a few games of Subbuteo. Dale's team was Peru or the *'Boyzees!'* as he would call them. They were a South American team wearing White shirts with a diagonal Red stripe and white shorts. Steve's team was also South American. Uruguay. They had pale blue shirts and black shorts. They played each other all the time and Dale reckoned he and Steve were fairly evenly matched.

So there we were at work, chatting away about Subbuteo with each one of us claiming we were the best when Chubby-Dodds declared that there would be only one way to settle this and that would be to have a tournament.

Now we were all in excitement about this challenge. A Tournament! I'd never played in a tournament before – well, other than with Terry and Laurence and my neighbours, but this? A real, proper, full-blown tournament, played by adults? Great! So we all chipped-in with some money and Dale went down the road to Beatties (it was still there!) and bought a trophy. A Subbuteo replica of the Jules Rimet World Cup trophy no less. Wow! This just suddenly became serious. I was up for winning that.

But first, I needed to practice...

Peru

Chapter 4.
At Chubby's.

And practice I did. That weekend, I enlisted the help of Laurence after explaining everything to him, we played a few games. I got Chile out and he played as West Germany and although it had been a few years since I'd last played – even longer for Laurence – I found that I hadn't really lost any of my old silky skills and deft touches. I was a little rusty in the first couple of games but that soon wore off and practically won every game we played. Sufficiently satisfied that I was ready, Monday morning couldn't come quickly enough when we would sort everything out.

Back in work on Monday, it turned out that everyone had been practicing over the weekend which only served to heighten the excitement. T-Dubs took great delight in teasing everyone about the event. He would make comments like "Don't forget to warm you fingers first lads..." and then sit on his hands and fart! Then he'd say "Oops! Nearly had to call for the trainer there, I almost followed-through with that one!" Or he walk past our section on his way to the typing pool, limbering-up by stretching and flexing his index fingers

saying "One, two, three, one, two, three..."
All good-natured banter.

At lunch, we trundled down to the
Catherine Wheel pub over the road from work
and ironed out a few of the rules. A referee
would be appointed to each match. We'd play
for 10 minutes each-way and _DEFINITELY_
flicking the players in the correct manner
allowed only, so I was happy. We fixed a date
for the following week and were all set to play
one night after work.

Dale, Clint, Sedge and I met up at
Chubby's house in Norbury. Sure enough, he had
a stadium. He had a specially converted table
which had an MDF top. It was very smooth and
very flat. I also noticed that he'd also
flattened the pitch as well. He was dead-proud
of the _smoothness_ of his pitch. He said he
regularly ran a warm iron over it to keep it
like that. In fact, he had overdone it as was
more like a thin green bed sheet stretched over
the table. It was completely bald and devoid
of any small hairs or fibres. This meant that
there was no natural spring from the table and
that the ball would run a lot faster than I
was used to.

Bordering the pitch, Chubby had installed
the Subbuteo pitch surround fencing which also
helped to keep the ball and players on the

table. All-in-all, it was quite a good little set-up.

So there we were, all set. Chubby was going to be Sweden, Clint Belgium, Sedge West Germany and Dale brought his *Boyzees*, Peru. I ... didn't use Chile. I chickened-out and had brought a couple of other teams and used one of those instead.

Before we started, we thought that we'd better review the game rules. After all, the *real* Subbuteo rules were flaky at best and open to interpretation, or *mis-interpretation* as I'd often found when playing friends. Local rules ruled! Which was rather disappointing as you'd expect the manufacturers to sort this aspect of the game out but - as I was to learn later in life when I bought a book about Subbuteo - they hadn't. Even Terry, whom I'd relied upon to read and understand the rules when I was eight and he nineteen, had failed to interpret them properly. So, he made up *additional* rules to suit his style of play and then *omitted* others that didn't suit or were a bit complex to understand.

So it was a good idea to agree and sort them in advance and The rules were generally agreed as follows:

- A maximum of three flicks per playing figure before he had to 'pass' the ball or allow another player on the same team to take possession. (You took possession by hitting the ball with a player).

- If you either missed the ball or hit it but it then rolled and touched a player from the opposing team last, then possession passed to your opponent.

- You had to 'flick' the players. There would be no scraping, dragging or pushing of players – as per Terry's technique.

- It would be a foul, penalized by either a free-kick or penalty if inside the penalty area if the player you flicked missed the ball but touched an opponent. Even if your player hit the ball after touching an opponent, it would still be a foul. (This rule would come into play later.) If it was a direct free-kick (i.e. inside the shooting area) the defender was also allowed to pick up and place three players to form a 'wall'. These players had to be no nearer than 3" (75mm) from the ball. Then both the attacking player and then the defender could flick up to three players into attacking/defensive positions.

- You were also allowed to move up to three men for corners and goal-kicks, one for throw-ins. But again, you had to flick them into position, so if they rolled where you didn't want them – tough! The attacking side would move his three men first, then the defending side would flick to 'mark' the forwards.

- The time limit was ten minutes each way. Twenty minute games. However, this turned out to be too long and we had to revise this to seven minutes each way when it came to playing a full-on tournament.
- Players were not allowed to 'kick' the ball any further than three-quarters of

the length of the pitch.

This was easy to determine as the pitch was divided into quarters. This stopped you from kicking the ball the entire length of the pitch. Otherwise, regardless who touched it last, the possession would go to your opponent.

- You had to *'Defend your goal at all times!'* which meant that you did not have to wait for the defending goalkeeper to be set or ready before you shot at goal. If the defending player wasn't ready, again, it was TOUGH!
- You could not 'flick' your goalkeeper's handle or rod to make him 'run' out of his goal to simulate rushing out (another rule made up by Terry) to clear the ball.
- Goalkeepers could not gain possession if the ball touched them last like it did with outfield players.
- Goalkeepers could touch or hit a moving/ rolling ball to clear it away from the goal but once the ball stopped moving, they couldn't touch it – unless it was already your possession.

Everything was fine and everyone agreed with the rules. However, there was one rule which Dale *insisted* upon – and which no-one else objected to but caused me no end of grief – was the size of the ball.

Now Subbuteo used to manufacture three sizes of ball. The first (White) was so large compared to the players it may as well have been a Ping-Pong ball. It was ridiculously over-sized but was made to help the beginner get to grips with the game.

The second type of ball (Yellow) was smaller (though still large by comparison) was an intermediate type of ball which still held a bit of weight to it but was quite comfortable (for me anyway) to control. Now, I had used this type of ball for years and years and was completely used to how it played. The third type of ball (Orange) was the smallest and lightest type produced and was normally only found with the Subbuteo 5-A-Side set which was sold and was made so small and light as to reproduce the speed and thrills of 5-A-Side football.

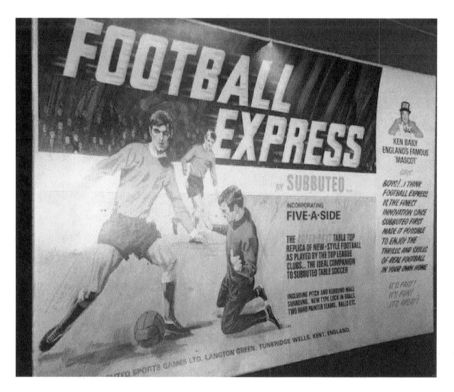

Although I had this set, I had never really used this type of ball outside of the 5-A-Side set and *never* on a full sized pitch. So I didn't know how it behaved or how to control it. Dale on the other hand was a past-master of it and absolutely insisted we used it. As I said, no-one else objected so I was outnumbered. The small ball it was. What could be the harm...? However, as you can see, size matters! The small ball was made for the Five-A-Side set as the goals were too small for the intermediate size ball.

So, rules sorted and all set for the first match of the evening: Clint versus Chubby, Belgium versus Sweden with Dale refereeing, we kicked off.

Standing there, beer in hand I was able to assess the relative playing strengths of both Clint and Chubby. Chubby was clearly the stronger player and he went on to win Two – One but Clint was no slouch either. However, I was confident that I could beat both of them and probably the other two as well.

The next game was decided and it would be me versus Dale and his *Boyzees*. As for me, I'd chickened out from playing with my team, Chile – just in case I lost – and instead played with

Brazil. They looked magnificent on that summer's evening with the bright sunlight coming in the French windows at Chubby's house. Brazil, playing in their gold shirts and blue shorts were against Dale's Peru in their all-white strip with distinctive diagonal red stripe. What a match this would be...

The match kicked-off with Clint refereeing. I was instantly struck by two things: First of all, my formation was CRAP!

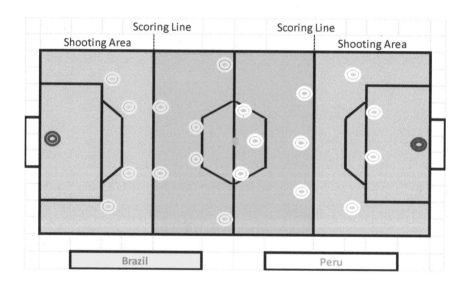

I'd been using a 4-2-4 setup since the dawn of time and Dale was using the far more solid 4-3-3 setup. What it exposed instantly was that I had relatively no mid-field just two players, and that two of my forwards — the wingers - were instantly out of the game. They were just far too wide. So this allowed Dale to sail straight through and attack my goal and I was immediately under pressure in the first five or ten seconds having to save his first shot!

The second thing I'd noticed was the *speed* of the ball. I just couldn't control it. Chubby's pitch was *so* flat and *so* smooth and *so bald* that with this smaller, lightweight ball, there were no fibres on the cloth to stop it rolling. Therefore, I was over-hitting my passes. The ball would just roll out of touch or go for a goal kick or simply be too long or too far from any of my own men. So when that happened it meant I had to flick my men harder and further to catch the ball. But when I did, their momentum was too hard and would just knock the ball out. Now as Chubby's pitch was so hard and so smooth on the MDF base, my men just slid or bounced around the pitch either missing the ball or just crashing into Dale's players giving away possession and free-kicks! It was like I was playing on ice and had no control over my men.

Dale on the other hand was very well at ease with this pitch and played comfortably and easily and was certainly better on it than I was.

Then, about halfway through the first half, Dale came though into my penalty area on my left-hand side. I went to move my goalkeeper out next to the ball but thought he would just whack the ball against my 'keeper and it would go out for a corner. So, thinking strategically

– or so I thought – I kept my 'keeper near my left-hand post, just angled at 45° so if the ball hit him, it would stay in play. Well, that was the plan anyway.

Dale carefully took aim, angled his finger slightly, then flicked... and the ball sailed over my keeper and went just inside my right-hand post for a goal! One – Nil!

"Boyzees!" He shouted and danced a little jig around the table. I was amazed. I had never seen anyone play a shot like it! He of course, knew what to expect. It was the ball. Being so light he was easily able to make it lift. I, having never used it before, didn't expect this to happen and was caught off guard. This match

was going to be harder than I thought.

The second half was pretty much the same as the first. I was struggling for control of the ball whilst Dale was gliding effortlessly around the table and with only a few minutes left on the clock disaster struck! Dale had been coaxing the ball skilfully through the midfield when he slightly overran the ball with his player and he missed it. The ball and Dale's player were close together and just inside my defensive shooting line. It was my turn to flick but I didn't have any players near to the ball, so I chose one which was in my penalty area, took aim and carefully flicked him. Unfortunately for me, playing on such a super-fast, hard surface as this my flick was poor and sent my man skittling past the ball and straight into Dale's man.

"Phweep!" Blew Clint on the whistle – yes, we had a whistle.

"Free kick!" he announced.

Now the fact that the player I'd fouled was within my shooting line meant that it was a *direct* free kick which meant that he could shoot directly at my goal. Worse still, the foul had occurred just off centre to my goal so it was in the perfect place for him to shoot from.

I set up my defensive three-man-wall three inches back from the ball – this represented the "ten yard" rule – and Dale flicked his men into position. I flicked my defenders accordingly. Dale set himself to flick, I braced myself to move my 'keeper, Clint blew his whistle... Dale flicked...

"GOAL*!*" Shouted Dale.

"Goal!" declared Clint and Dale was again running around the table, chanting "*Boyzees! Boyzees!...*" in celebration.

He had flicked a magnificent shot which made the ball rise up, skim the heads of my players in the wall and zip past my flailing goalkeeper into the top of my net. What a shot! Two – Nil.

Chubby then turned-up the stereo full blast to simulate the noise of the crowd.

"It's gone innnn!!!!" He shouted. "What a goal by Thorners and Peru. There's no way back for Dunny-boy and Brazil now!" in his best 'Motty' commentary.

The game ended shortly after and I was in a daze. I had not been so comprehensively beaten or outplayed since, well, ever! Well, in years at least anyway.

Dale of course was as smug as ever and had a huge grin on his face. And every now and then, throughout the rest of the evening he would look at me and chant "Boyzees! Boyzees! Boyzees!..." just to rub it in.

The rest of the evening continued with Chubby beating Sedge, me beating Clint - I had unleashed Chile for this match! - and Dale beating both Chubby and Sedge.

My next game was against Chubby and I was confident my Chile could beat his Sweden.

The game started and I quickly got on top, mounting wave after wave of attacks. Chubby defended well but by half-time I was leading Two - Nil and cruising. The second half started and by this time I had relaxed and was coasting to an easy victory when all of a sudden, Chubby mounted a very good counter-attack, came

through the middle, shot and scored! "Goal!!!!
Whoah Turkington!! It's gone in!!!!!" he
cried! "Two - One!"

Unfortunately for me, whether it was the
beer or it was just getting a bit late or
whatever, I just couldn't snap out of cruise-
control and with the tide of the game turning
in Chubby's favour, it was all I could do to
keep him out. And buoyed by his success, with
just a couple of minutes left on the clock,
Chubby broke through on the right with a strong
attack down the wing, cut inside the defender
and made an excellent shot past my 'keeper.

"Two - Two!" Shouted Chubby. "Whoahhh!!!
Turkington again!" and this time, instead of
re-setting his men, he ran to the stereo and
turned it up FULL BLAST again.
'SCHHHHHHhhhhhh!!!!' went the white noise
"...and the crowd's gone wild!" shouted
Chubby. "They just can't stop the boy
Turkington!"

The match eventually resumed but
fortunately for me he'd wasted valuable
seconds mucking about with his celebrations
and after surviving the last minute-or-so
under great pressure I was relieved to hear
the tinny rattle of his game timer signalling
the end of the match.

What a relief! But it was so unnecessary. I should have had the game wrapped up at half-time instead of letting it slip to a Two - All draw. I had a two goal lead! I should have finished him off. "I won't let *that* happen again." I thought to myself. But it does...

Unfortunately, one of the things we hadn't given any thought to before the evening started was a proper order of play or work out how long it was all going to take. We'd turned up at Chubby's ready to play but not realising that twenty minute games were going to take too long and before we knew it, it was getting late and we still had a couple of games left to play. Chubby had had enough by this point and wanted us to wrap things up. Dale agreed and reminded us all that we still had work the next day. He also said that as Chubby and I had beaten Clint and he had beaten us, it was obvious to him that he would also beat Clint and therefore didn't need to play him. Sedge was a novice by comparison and therefore would lose his next game as well and so we didn't need to play anymore. Therefore, Dale declared himself the clear winner.

Chapter 5.
A Two-legged Affair.

The next day Dale was strutting around the office like a Peacock! His walk had an extra bit of *bounce* to it and he had the biggest grin on his face you could imagine. He was parading the *"Boyzees!"* and telling everyone about how he'd won the competition by "thrashing everyone" he'd played.

"What a smug git!" I thought. And he rubbed it in all day. Eventually, I could stand it no longer and I challenged him to another match. This time it would be his *Boyzees* Peru against my top team Chile.

Well that was it. Gauntlet thrown!

"And to make it more interesting," I said "let's make it a two-legged affair: home and away matches with away goals counting double!" My reasoning behind it was two-fold; if we were as closely matched as I'd believed and *he* won the first leg, I'd at least get the chance to fight him back in the second. Or so I thought. It never occurred to me that I might lose both matches. My second reason was that I also fancied playing an 'away' match at an 'away' venue i.e. on *his* pitch.

So there it was. A two-legged match-up with Peru vs. Chile set for the following week-or-so (I was evasive as I'd wanted time to practice with these damned nuisance balls!) and we'd agreed that whenever it was, Tuesdays were best for both of us. We tossed a coin to see who played 'away' for the first leg and Dale won. It made sense really as I only lived just down the road from the office and he could easily bring his *Boyzees* into work.

I managed to rope in Laurence and spent as much time as I could fit in practicing with this new ball. By now, I was starting to get to grips with it whilst Laurence struggled - as I had at Chubby's house. Laurence didn't win a single game and I was beginning to feel confident that I could beat Dale.

Eventually, 'match day Tuesday' rolled around and Dale brought in the *Boyzees*. There was a real buzz in the office that day. The banter had been building all the previous week and the Monday before. There was much debate as to who would win and what the scores were going to be. Even Edna, the elderly tea-lady (whom we used to call '*Edna Bucket*' - Eva never did understand the joke - she used to push a tea-trolly and large urn of boiling water, dispensing cups of tea and coffee around the office - another Health & Safety nightmare!) even she knew all about it and wished us both well. "And may the best man win," and all that old rubbish. But secretly, she wanted *me* to win. "give him one for me..." she said. Well, I think I knew what she meant by that remark but who knew the powers of his charm. I mean, I know she was nearly seventy but she was still a woman after all...

Now Tuesdays was always a bit of a funny day. It wasn't the beginning of the week and it was almost as far away from the weekend as you could get. The last one was well and truly history and the next one so far into the distance you couldn't see it. So on a Tuesday, Sedge would see his girlfriend *'Debs'* as that was "their day". Or night as the case may be. You see, although we all worked in the same building and they saw each other almost every single day at work, they only saw each other on a Tuesday night during the week so things didn't get stale. They wanted to keep their relationship 'fresh'. Well, that's what Debs kept telling him anyway. The reality was, she wanted the rest of the week to go out with her girlfriends *pulling* behind his back! But Sedge was in love – or so he thought – and he let her rule the roost and have it all her own way. If she wanted to do something, she did it. For example: She went on a week long holiday with her girlfriends to Greece that summer. However, If he wanted to do something, he had to check with her first. And on *this* night, she said "No".

"But Dunny-boy and Thorners are playing their big match tonight!" wailed Sedge.

"It's only Subbuteo," She said, "besides, I can't believe you'd rather see them playing a kid's game, than come round to mine..."

"But you're only gonna be washing your hair, you told me..." he whined.

Now, to be fair to Debs she did have a gorgeous mane of long, wavy, lush, blonde hair that needed a lot of attention to keep it in that fabulous, 'natural' condition.

"Yes," she purred, "but then you can help me *wash* it... in the shower... mum and dad are going out. They won't be back for hours..."

Well, that was it. He was on a promise!

Women! See how devious they can be?

Clint wasn't any better. Although his promise was for his mum to cook his tea. To be fair to him, he lived a few miles out of town and had to get the bus home. It wasn't always a reliable service back then so when his mum offered him a lift home he accepted it. Plus, his mum used to give him grief if he got home late for his tea on a work night. Well, he was only eighteen and straight out of college.

Chubby was also a let-down. He had gone off sick that day. We never knew if he really was sick or just throwing a dodgy 'sicky' just to bunk off work for a day as he often used to do that and then brag about it later. I was really surprised no-one ever pulled him up about it but he just didn't care and got away with it.

So there it was, no-one to cheer us on.

Ah well, I would just have to tell them all about my glorious victory in the morning...

Straight after work Dale drove us to my house in his little mustard coloured MG sports car. It was his pride and joy. It was the middle of summer and we had the roof down "with the wind in our hair..." as my mother used to say. In fact, she used to tease and irritate me with that little phrase as it was a reference to my next-door-neighbour Stephen and his younger brother Danny.

Stephen was born six months after me and had his birthday in the September, which meant that he was in the year below me at school. However, when we were kids, he was big for his age. He was slightly bigger and certainly stronger than me. And as we got older, he continued to grow and he became quite a big strong lad and so did his brother. Mother always used to compare us.

"He's bigger than you and he's younger. I'll bet Danny will be bigger than you in a couple of years too. Why is that? Is it because they go to bed early and get up early, running around that garden with the wind in their hair and the roses in their cheeks..."

"No mother," I would *think* of saying but never actually dared voice it "it's because their dad is six foot seven and twenty-odd stone for Christ's sakes! Our dad was only five foot six, you do the math. It's called *genetics*!"

And relax...

Anyway, when we got to my house, Dale charmed my mother as he did with all the ladies he met. How did he do it? Mum never liked anyone I brought home. Male or female. But she liked him, _and_ she made him a cup of tea! So after a polite chat and a cuppa with my mum, we went into the front room to do battle.

My table was already set up and looking like a stadium with the floodlights and score board and Dale was suitably impressed. He was so impressed with the table that he wanted to play Snooker instead. I said "No." as we had unfinished business...

Now this time I didn't chicken out. I brought out my team Chile and set them up in a revised 4-2-4 formation, which basically moved my wingers in nearer the centre circle and back slightly with my two mid-fielders spreading to plug the gaps. "We'll see if this works any better" I thought.

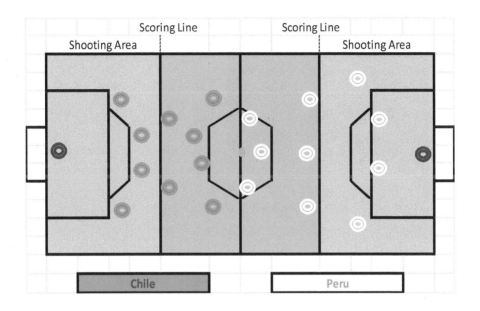

I also had a change of goalkeeper.

Now Dale's goalkeeper was of the more modern, 'lightweight' variety where his arms were spread out in a 'Y' shape and his body was straight with his chest slightly forward. I didn't have one of these types. The more usual 'heavyweight' type of diving goalkeeper I had was moulded with his hands closer together and was diving slightly to one side. So, because I didn't have one of the new styles of goalkeeper, I decided to go completely old-

 school and use a very old one. I used a crouching goalkeeper that came from my original Red & Blue boxed set and he was ever-so-slightly bigger than normal and came on a metal rod which was removable. Now this rod was about an inch-and-a-quarter longer than the plastic ones. So this meant that not only was he bigger, he could stretch out of his goal further – almost to the penalty spot – but more than that, he also had the advantage of being removable from the rod if I needed to use him to kick the ball away. In other words, he could be an extra defender as well.

So Dale's keeper had height and wide arms and my keeper had reach and a wider stance. Fair enough I thought.

Dale looked at my 'keeper with an accusing eye. "You can't use that!" He said. "That's cheating!"

"No it isn't" I said. "It's a Subbuteo figure and therefore it must be legal" and I showed him the other goalkeeper for the Blue team. "Look, here's another". That shut him up.

We tossed a coin for ends and kick-off, which Dale won, and we got the game underway.

My revised formation, coupled with my additional practice with the smaller ball was paying off. Also, having the advantage of playing on my home pitch was working well and within a few minutes, I had broken through with my number 8 who shot from the edge of his penalty area and the ball screamed into the back of his net! Easy. "One – Nil!" I shouted, grinning from ear-to-ear. This time it was going to be different. I could *feel* it.

Dale kicked off and it was the usual cut 'n' thrust; he'd attack, break down, then I'd attack, break down. On it went until just over half-way through the first half, Dale caught me in my own half. I lost possession, he ran through to a similar position to that from where I'd scored and he equalised! "Boyzees!" He cried! "One – One, Game on!"

I kicked off and was putting his defence under pressure again when I gave the ball away just inside his scoring area. Dale skilfully manoeuvred his player to the ball and cleared it. Now the ball was resting on his own scoring line at this point but *more* of it was resting in the 'middle area' of the pitch i.e. <u>not</u> in his own shooting area.

Anyway, his player kicked the ball and it rolled all the way to my shooting area.

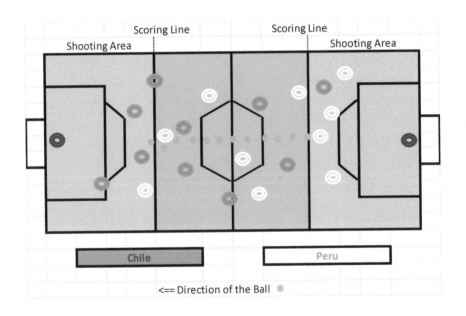

However, just as it got there it faintly touched another one of his players who was standing on the shooting line and then the ball rolled into my shooting area. Now the rules state that you can't kick from one shooting area to the next without the ball touching another player on the way. Otherwise, the defending team gets automatic possession. This is to stop unrealistic long-balls constantly happening.

Now this ball was literally border-line to begin with, as it was on the line when he kicked it. And it was just the faintest, merest of touches when it hit his player before rolling into my danger area. And *because* it was so border-line, Dale wasn't sure if he should carry on and take possession. He thought he'd over-hit the ball, groaned and pulled a face.

I *could* have just taken that as my cue to attack the ball and clear it but, I'd like to think of myself as an honest player - and this gets put to the test later on – but I felt that the ball had fairly and legally, hit his player on the base before it rolled into my shooting area. So I said "No, no, it's ok. It's your ball, go on. It's fair..." <u>What</u>?! *What was I saying*? He had actually hit a *brilliant* pass but it was just <u>so</u> border-line he was letting me have the benefit of the doubt. Yet I go and say "No. Here, <u>you</u> have it. You have an opportunity to score!" What a TWAT! Even today in professional football the referee usually gives the defence the benefit of the doubt.

Well, Dale didn't need a second invitation. He lined his player up behind the ball and slammed it into the back of my net! Two - One. Boy was I sick. And boy, did I deserve it. However, funnily enough, for the first time when scoring a goal he didn't shout "Boyzees!" He just said "Goal!" and set his men up ready for the re-start.

As I said, I felt sick as the proverbial parrot and I think perhaps he wasn't too keen on scoring the goal like that. There had been too much ambiguity about it.

But there it was; Two - One to Dale at half time.

We changed ends and I kicked off. By now I was getting back into the swing of the match again and started to batter his defences. I managed to win a corner kick and placed my men into attacking positions. I crossed the ball, took one pass from one player and with my No. 9 standing by the penalty spot spanked the ball past his 'keeper. "Goal!" I cried. "Two - Two!" The game was on and there was plenty of time for a winner...

And the winner did come... although sadly not to me.

Halfway through the second half, Dale again pierced my defence and he beat my keeper with a low hard shot into the back of my net.

This time, there was the fanatical cry of "Boyzees!" and he was off, bouncing round the table again doing a little jig.

I was getting pretty sick of the sound of his bloody "Boyzees!" by this time and again pressed forward hard for an equalizer that never came. Bugger! Beaten 3-2 in a thriller of a match by a dodgy – well, not really – goal, which I then moaned like hell about once the game was over. Just like a losing football manager does on '*Match of the day*' as he complains about the poor refereeing decisions that went against his team.

"You accepted it at the time, you should've said something!" argued Dale. And he was right. It was the equivalent of a dodgy offside decision going against the defence. If I'd appealed at the time or just played my shot when Dale clearly thought he'd knocked the ball too far, the game might have ended up a draw. But I didn't and I was beaten for a second time.

Chapter 6.
Didn't have a leg to stand on.

The next day at work, Dale was intolerable.

He was bragging to everyone and anyone who would listen – because by now, half the bloody company knew about Subbuteo and our "big match".

He was just simply *gloating* and rubbing it in, and every single time he passed by me he would shout or whisper or chant "Boyzees!! Boyzees!! Boyzees!!" or remind me of the score "Three – Two, Three – Two, Three – Two!!"

How bloody irritating!

I just had to sit there and take it. Oh, how that smarted, and he *knew* it. The smug git.

Every now and then, even T-Dubs would come up and say, "What was the score again chaps?..." just to get Dale going again, or "You'd better win the second game Dunny-boy or...you won't have a _leg_ to stand on! Ha, ha, ha!" Oh, how *very* bloody funny - not!

A couple of weeks' passed and we tried to re-arrange the second leg of the match where he would be the 'home' side but we never actually managed to do it. That is, we could never arrange a time for me to get over to his club in Bexley to play. So in the meantime, Dale was enjoying the banter and the ribbing he was inflicting on me. Of course, all this did was to push Subbuteo to the fore-front of everyone's mind again and this time a full blown 'World Cup' tournament was proposed. This would include everyone; Me, Sedge, Chubby, Clint and of course Dale. Dale even hinted at getting his mate Steve to play as well. More the merrier I thought – especially if it was someone who could possibly BEAT him – so that was a plus.

Eventually, Dale suggested playing his home leg back at my house, otherwise we would never get the two-legged match over with before the *World Cup* – and he definitely wanted to establish dominance over me before *that* tournament started.

So, back to my house it was and *this* time I wasn't going to be 'Mr Nice Guy'. If there were any ambiguous moments, then I would stand my ground and argue my corner. He'd been cut enough slack already and I was determined I wouldn't lose for a third match in a row!

Yet again, it was a nice, warm, sunny evening when Dale came round. I'd made excuses earlier in the day saying I had to do something before going home so could he "hang around for half-an-hour-or-so before turning up?" This meant that I could get the bus home without travelling with him in his car as I didn't want to have to pass any pleasantries with him and instead just psyched myself up for the battle ahead.

Mentally prepared, I waited for Dale to arrive. I'd primed mum that I wasn't inviting him in for tea and chit-chat, this was to be an all-or-nothing evening where I *had* to win! No distractions.

The doorbell rang and I let mum answer it so she could say "hello" and she led Dale into the front room. Sunshine poured in through the French windows and the table was bathed in glorious light. There was no need for the 'floodlights' to be on this time.

We set our teams up as per normal and tossed a coin for the kick-off, which I won and the game started.

Having been taunted and ridiculed for the past three or four weeks I was determined more than ever to have my revenge and I went full-pelt at Dale's defences. I could beat him, of that I was certain. I just had to prove it.

And during the first half, after some sustained pressure by me the breakthrough came. The ball was manoeuvred through the middle of the pitch and out to the left. My captain, *'El Capitán'* the Chile number 11 passed an inch-perfect ball to my number 10 just inside Dale's scoring area and he (well, me, actually) smashed the ball into the roof of his net! One - Nil and Three - Three on aggregate. I had scored a valuable away goal. One more from me and as long as he didn't score, that would be that, I would be the winner! And over *TWO* legs as well.

The second half was a very, *very* close-fought affair with numerous chances for both sides, near misses, great saves but sadly, no more goals.

This meant that with the score all-tied at three goals each the 'away goals rule' would come into play.

And away goals counted for Double...

So the scores were:-

1st leg:

Chile 2 vs 3* Peru (*count double = **6**)

2nd leg:

Peru 0 vs 1* Chile (*count double = **2**)

This didn't look good...

Total:

Chile (4) 3 - 3 (6) Peru

Peru win on aggregate.

Bugger!

This meant that despite *winning* against him on the night and despite the fact that I had still scored *exactly* the same number of goals (3) as him, Dale STILL won. Bugger again! How the bloody hell did that happen? It was *so* unfair! I mean, the margin for this win was so close. For example: If Dale had *not* won the toss for the first match and couldn't chose to be the 'away' team and had played at 'home' instead, then the scores would have looked like this:-

1st leg:

Peru 3 vs 2* Chile (*count double = **4**)

2nd leg:

Chile 1 vs 0* Peru (*count double = **0**)

And the results would have looked like this...

Total:

Chile (5) 3 - 3 (3) Peru

So I would have been the winner! But more than that; *IF* that 'dodgy' goal Dale scored from the first leg had not have happened then the scores would have been:-

1st leg:

Chile 2 vs 2 Peru

2nd leg:

Peru 0 vs 1 Chile

There is no need to count 'away' goals as the match overall would not have been drawn and therefore the final score would have been...

Total:

Chile 3 – 2 Peru

I would have won 3-2(on aggregate) so you can see *just how close* it was.

But Dale didn't see.

And neither did anyone else. It just seemed to them that I was being a sour-graped, bad loser. And perhaps I was. I just couldn't seem to beat him.

And yet, I *had* beaten him, at least in the second-leg. He couldn't deny that. *AND* he hadn't scored either, no matter how hard he'd tried. So there were two very big pluses for

me and this was just a couple of weeks-or-so
before the big one, *The World Cup*. We would
see who was going to be a sour-graped bad loser
then!

Chapter 7.
The World Cup 1981.

The following week-or-so was spent by me practicing hard at home and trying to decide which of my teams I should enter. Of course, I *wanted* to enter Chile but the truth of the matter was that I just couldn't bear the thought of losing with them. True, they had inflicted defeat on Dale's "Boyzees!" but I <u>had</u> lost overall (on the away goals rule as previously explained) in the two-legged affair.

But I also wanted to show-off a little. I wanted people to see that I had a number of teams I could choose from. I wasn't stuck with just one or two, and I couldn't quite decide who I wanted to play as.

There were a few candidates:

1. Chile
2. Brazil — Nah, they'd already been comprehensively beaten or...
3. Holland.

I had a couple of other reasonable choices available to me; England, Scotland, West Germany and a couple of other club teams that could have doubled-up as an 'international' team but I wanted something... different.

Now, over the years, I'd accumulated several spare or reserve players from one source or another and shortly after the actual 1978 World Cup in Argentina, I'd painted these spare players with orange shirts and white shorts to create 'Holland'. At the time, they briefly overtook the No.1 spot from Chile as my favourite team as I'd created them and they were completely unique in their appearance. They were made up from a mix of the types of players you could get in Subbuteo. For example; there was the standard *Heavyweight* player, a Walker/*winged-shorts* type of player, a *lightweight* type and a *zombie* type (from a 5-a-side set).

And there was one I had which, well, I wasn't quite sure where he came from. I later learned that he was a figure from something called *TAF Grandstand 4-2-4* although I must admit I'm not too sure exactly what type of football game that is.  Anyway, this particular player was ever-so-slightly taller than the normal standard player and he was in a *running-style* pose as opposed to the normal Subbuteo stance. He had no base but I had a spare one from a broken player and stuck him on it instead and when he was painted, he looked magnificent! He <u>had</u> to be my Centre Forward. A big No.9.

Another player I was very fond of in this team was the left-winger. He was a spare player, clad all in light blue (Coventry City I later learned) and he was quite well balanced and could spin really well. I was able to control him better than most of the players I had in my entire collection. I know they all *should* play the same but some just don't and others well, they simply stand out... and he did.

He was so good, I thought I'd distinguish him from all of the other No. 11's (Left-Wingers) I had so when I painted the numbers on their backs I painted No. 21 on his. You see, even back then I was leading edge! Squad numbers not just 1 - 11 but 1 - what-ever-you-liked. Well, '21' in this case.

The goalkeeper was also another good choice. He was from a boxed set of six 'keepers that Subbuteo did. He was a *straight* - not curved - diving goalkeeper and he was dressed all in white. He made a perfect contrast to the orange and white of the out-field players and finished the team off nicely.

How grand they all looked! (to my eyes.)

So there it was. Holland would be my choice of team. I liked them and they played well. They were an excellent choice of team to take to *The World Cup*. Looking at them now though, through the eyes of a middle-aged adult they were not that brilliantly painted...

However, it did ensure that there would be no problem of team colours clashing that's for sure. Clint was going to play Belgium and they wore Red shirts with Black shorts. My Chile had Red shirts with Blue shorts. You could tell the difference but that was my excuse for changing the team.

At work, Dale confirmed that his mate and 'Subbuteo buddy' would also be participating in the hostilities, entering his team Uruguay. Fantastic! Another South American Team. Dale said it was to help "spice things up a bit" as he needed a bit of decent competition to keep him motivated... Clearly, it was a dig at me and that he thought I wasn't good enough. I could have punched his smug, bloody face in.

Another surprise was that Chubby-Dodds had decided not to play. Unfortunately, he waited until the day of the tournament to drop out. I couldn't understand it. Here was a lad who was mad-keen on football and absolutely bonkers into Subbuteo yet he was withdrawing his Sweden due to "other commitments". Yeah, right! The real reason was that he knew he wasn't good enough to win half of the matches and as he was a really sore loser anyway, he didn't want to run the risk of showing himself up if he lost too many matches. I mean, I could understand the not wanting to *lose* but to not take part at all... well, that was just plain mad. Still, as I didn't particularly much like him anyway, I wasn't overly sad to see him drop out but it did affect the tournament set-up and as a result, had far-reaching consequences on the outcome.

Originally, we were going to play *Group Stages* i.e. two groups of three and the top two teams go through to the *Knock-out Stage* with the winners' of each group playing the runners-up, in a *Semi-Final*. Then the winners would go on to contest the *Final*. Just like a proper world cup tournament. But Chubby's withdrawal meant that we only had five participants. So we had to settle for an "all-play-all" format. In hindsight, if I'd have known he was going to drop out, I could have invited my brother Laurence to take his place. But in the days of pre-mobile phones, there was no way I could have asked Laurence to join us in time as he worked in London. And anyway, we would have had to have waited for him to come home, have his dinner and then make his way to Clint's. Unfortunately, there was just no time to get him involved.

Anyway, one final bit of preparation for the tournament was to organise the order of matches before the evening. We'd failed to do this at Chubby's house and had ended-up with a hap-hazard order of play and not everyone got to play everyone. This time, in order to have an outright winner everyone had to play everyone. We also had to work out roughly what time to start and how long each of the games was going to last. If there was going to be say, ten matches, we needed to know how long it was all going to take. We drew lots for numbers and then drew numbers out of a hat – Sherlock had lent us his deerstalker for the occasion – and Jo and Sharon paraded round like the girls you see holding the ring cards at boxing matches and drew out the numbers.

So, there we were, same rules as at Chubby's house applied. However, the matches would be seven minutes each half with a one minute rest at half time. Therefore, each match lasted roughly a quarter-of-an-hour. We could get three matches per hour played, with changing teams over. There were ten games to get through. It should take only three-and-a-half hours if we kept to the schedule. We couldn't finish too late anyway, it was Clint's parents' house after all.

Unfortunately, we couldn't start the tournament until approximately 7:00pm as we had to wait for Steve to arrive from London after work – then we had to wait for Clint's mum and dad to finish their evening meal to free up the dining table. However, with strict adherence to the schedule, we could be still be finished by 11:00pm and maybe have time to go for a celebratory beer somewhere for the winner!

Perfect.

The players and teams taking part would be:-

(Listed in no particular order)

1. Ashley (well, I had to come top sometime 😊) - **Holland**
2. Dale - **Peru**
3. Clint - **Belgium**
4. Sedge - **West Germany*** (Note: *This was at a time when Germany was split between East and West)
5. Steve - **Uruguay**

The order of play was to be as follows:-

1. **West Germany vs Uruguay**
2. **Belgium vs Peru**
3. **Holland vs West Germany**
4. **Belgium vs Uruguay**
5. **Peru vs Holland**
6. **West Germany vs Belgium**
7. **Peru vs Uruguay**
8. **Belgium vs Holland**
9. **West Germany vs Peru**

The last game of the night would be Steve vs me.

10. Uruguay vs Holland

So the weekend before the tournament, I enlisted the help of Laurence again for practice and this time I invited Clint round for a game or two as well. He could do with the practice I told him. It was also a good morale boost for me as I thrashed them both three and four nil in practically every game. Only in one game did Laurence go close at two - one. Clint never even scored. Not even against Laurence.

The following week passed and the hype and tension built up at work. There was lots of banter flying around our department, especially when the likes of Sherlock and T-Dubs joined in the banter - mainly poking fun at us all for being such sad geeks!

Anyway, the big day arrived and there was much excitement in the office. We were all clock-watching and counting down the hours until five O'clock when we could race out of work, get home for a quick change and race up to Clint's house.

This particular evening, Sedge was coming round to my house to pick me up in his car - it was the least he could do as I was lending him West Germany again for the evening. I felt sorry for my poor team as I knew they were going to lose every match because Sedge wasn't as good as the rest of us. Hey, they're _NOT_ just pieces of moulded plastic I'm telling you, they have feelings too!

So there we were all sorted and finally congregated at Clint's parents' house which was a lovely big six bed-roomed, mock-Tudor style, detached house in Old Coulsdon. Their living room was a huge open-plan affair with a large seating area, large dining table – upon which sat the pitch and fence surrounds – and most importantly of all, a fridge in which to keep the beers cold in. Perfect.

The order of play meant that Sedge (playing as West Germany) would play Steve (Uruguay) with Dale refereeing would start the evening. This meant that Nigel and I could watch the first match from the side-lines and have a can of beer to settle the pre-match nerves.

However, things didn't quite go to plan as Steve didn't actually turn up until just after 7:30pm. This, don't forget was in the days before mobile phones so we didn't know just how late he was going to be and we agreed it was unfair to start playing without him when we knew he was coming. We also did not want to upset the running order, so we waited. By the time he'd turned up, got himself settled, said "hello" to everyone, got a beer, set his men up, we didn't actually start the first game of the tournament until well after 8:00pm. Our 11:00pm finish was now out of the window.

Game 1. West Germany Vs. Uruguay

 So kick-off started and the game followed a very predictable pattern of play. Steve was reasonably good and Sedge wasn't and as expected, Steve ran out a comfortable Two - Nil winner, scoring his first goal early on in the first half and then sealing his win with a second early in the second half.

Sedge rarely looked like troubling Steve's goal and in truth, Steve could probably have won by three or four goals but you could see he was just happy getting his first win under his belt. After all, he only had Dale's word for it just how good (or bad) we were.

Result: West Germany 0 - 2 Uruguay

The World Cup 1981
Standings after 1st Game

Teams	PLD	W	D	L	G/F	G/A	Diff	PTS
Uruguay	1	1	0	0	2	0	2	2
Belgium	0	0	0	0	0	0	0	0
Holland	0	0	0	0	0	0	0	0
Peru	0	0	0	0	0	0	0	0
W Germany	1	0	0	1	0	2	-2	0

Note: We were playing for **two points** for a win, one for a draw and zero for a loss. The three points for a win rule came into play in England around that time but was only introduced in the world Cup in 1994.

Game 2. Belgium Vs. Peru

The second match was between Clint (Belgium) and the pre-tournament favourites Dale and his '*Boyzees!*' (Peru).

Dale had not yet played Clint as we'd run out of time at Chubby's house due to a scheduling error – we hadn't worked out how long it was going to take to do an all-play-all tournament, so Dale didn't really know Clint's playing strength. He had seen him play but it's not quite the same thing. I, however, had played both enough times to realise Dale was certainly the far stronger player. I didn't hold out much hope...

However, what you *expect* to be the case and what actually _is_ the case may sometimes turn out to be completely different. Clint was actually playing a blinder! Rather unexpectedly, it was Dale who was struck by what can only be described as "pre-tournament nerves" and couldn't string two passes together. Clint on the other-hand having 'home pitch' advantage and had been expecting to lose, didn't have the same pressure thrust upon him and took full advantage of the way Dale was playing. He managed to manoeuvre the ball into Dale's scoring area and for the first time ever, took a nervous flick at Dale's goal.

"Goal!" cried Clint, though it was more of a surprise than a statement.

"Yes!" I shouted as I punched the air with delight.

"Goal"! Announced Steve and he pointed to the centre spot.

"I've scored!" said Clint, although this time with a little more conviction and he did a little hop, with one arm raised in the air. "I've scored!" he said again and did a little jig.

This was it! This was the big one. *The Subbuteo World Cup 1981*. And Clint, the lowly Belgium was one-nil up against pre-tournament favourites, Dale and his '*Boyzees*' the mighty Peru.

Like a championship boxer recovering from a first-round knockdown, Dale recovered his composure and dug deep. He battered Clint's defence. Shot after shot, pass and cross after pass and cross but to no avail. Clint's defence held! Eventually, the tinny sound of the half time bell rang and the score was still one - nil. Was a World Cup upset on the cards...?

They changed ends. The excitement buzzing through the air was electric. Dale had a manic look in his eyes as if to say "Right, you caught me with a lucky punch there matey, but now I'm coming to get you!" Clint on the other hand was just shocked he wasn't losing. Sedge and I were going crazy with excitement!

Dale kicked off for the second half applying lots of pressure to Clint's goal. Every flick and save from Clint was greeted with manic, over-the-top cheering from me and Sedge, whilst booing and jeering every one of Dale's. We cheered Clint on with shouts and noises of encouragement and just generally getting very, very excited about the fact that he was beating Dale. There were lots of "ooohs" and "ahhhs" at near misses for both players. It was great fun! God knows what the neighbours thought.

The tournament was really under-way now and Dale was feeling the pressure. Sedge and I were practically beside ourselves with the excitement! Cheering on Clint on and generally trying to put Dale off. The referee, Steve, had to warn us against "un-gentlemanly conduct" as we were getting just a little bit too rowdy and practically threatened to invade the pitch! (Just *how* we were going to do this without stepping on the players or breaking Clint's dinner table I don't know) but it was all good raucous fun and banter.

Sadly though, in spite of all our best efforts to play the partisan crowd and intimidate Dale, he managed to score an equalizer which shut us up for a bit. Bummer! One - All. Dale went off bouncing round the table, punching the air and shouting "Boyzees!" back in our faces.

However, it wasn't for long as almost straight away, Clint broke through and for the second time did the unthinkable... He scored again!

"Goal!" we all shouted. This time, Sedge and I mobbed him but Steve shouted at us and told us to get off him as the clock was still ticking. Dale was on the ropes! We were chanting "Two - one! Two - one! Two - one!" And every touch and flick of Dale's was booed whilst every touch of Clint's was met with great cheers! Back and forth went the action but in the final couple of minutes, Dale finally showed his class and scored the equalizer. Two - Two. Bugger!

The game ended shortly after and Dale had managed to salvage a point. For Clint, it was a point dropped but also an unexpected point gained as he had expected to lose. It was great fun - and thirsty work! Well played Clint. I needed another beer.

Result: Belgium 2 - 2 Peru

The World Cup 1981
Standings after 2nd Game

Teams	PLD	W	D	L	G/F	G/A	Diff	PTS
Uruguay	1	1	0	0	2	0	2	2
Belgium	1	0	1	0	2	2	0	1
Peru	1	0	1	0	2	2	0	1
Holland	0	0	0	0	0	0	0	0
W Germany	1	0	0	1	0	2	-2	0

<u>Game 3. Holland Vs. West Germany</u>

The third match of the night was between me and Sedge. West Germany as it was then versus my newly unveiled team of Holland. Now as I'd described earlier, this team was a home-made team which consisted of a collection of spares that were repainted and there were a few issues with this to say the least.

1. The paint job – not great. Back then, I thought they were ok and that I'd done a pretty good job of it. However, looking at them now they don't look so hot – rubbish actually. I obviously did not have a particularly steady hand... The players were all painted in the traditional Orange & White of Holland. The bases were also painted to match, but one or two – namely Dale and Steve – objected to this.

2. Dale particularly didn't like the look of my 'dodgy' no. 9 who was in a different stance to all the others. Really, he wanted me to play with Chile. However, common sense prevailed and my Holland was allowed to play.

Clint refereed and as expected, Dale – and Steve – took the opportunity for some revenge and sledge me.

Note: 'Sledging' is a term normally used in Cricket to describe the insults and abuse that the fielding side give to a batsman in order to try and put him off.

I got an absolute barrage from both of them – though more from Dale than Steve it must be said – but fair's fair, if you can't handle it, don't dish it, so I didn't complain. But it was very off-putting to say the least.

Sedge also played surprisingly well, even managing a shot on goal which I had to save and I had to endure more "Ooooh-ing" and "Aaahh-ing" from Dale and Steve. Eventually though, just before half-time I managed to score which helped to settle the nerves. That and the can of beer I was glugging. It was extremely warm in Clint's house and with all of the excitement, I was getting extremely thirsty...

The second half resumed with more banter and jeering from the crowd but I was able to silence them by swiftly scoring a second goal and taking full command of the match. Sedge never managed to threaten again and the partisan crowd calmed down and accepted the fact that I was going to win the match Two –

Nil and get my first two points on the board, thank you very much.

Result: Holland 2 - 0 West Germany

The World Cup 1981
Standings after 3rd Game

Teams	PLD	W	D	L	G/F	G/A	Diff	PTS
Holland	1	1	0	0	2	0	2	2
Uruguay	1	1	0	0	2	0	2	2
Belgium	1	0	1	0	2	2	0	1
Peru	1	0	1	0	2	2	0	1
W Germany	2	0	0	2	0	4	-4	0

Game 4. Belgium Vs. Uruguay

Game four was an altogether quieter affair with Steve once again putting in a very solid performance and as expected, beat Clint Two - Nil.

Result: Uruguay 2 - 0 Belgium

The World Cup 1981
Standings after 4th Game

Teams	PLD	W	D	L	G/F	G/A	Diff	PTS
Uruguay	2	2	0	0	4	0	4	4
Holland	1	1	0	0	2	0	2	2
Peru	1	0	1	0	2	2	0	1
Belgium	2	0	1	1	2	4	-2	1
W Germany	2	0	0	2	0	4	-4	0

Game five however, was about to bring the evening to life!

The Jules Rimet

World Cup Trophy

(Subbuteo version)

Chapter 8.
"What a match!"

Game 5. Peru Vs. Holland

 The fifth game of the tournament was the PURPLE patch of the evening. This was the game of the night! It was Dale versus me, me versus Dale. Peru versus Holland. My boys against his 'Boyzees!'

It was the match everyone was waiting to see. I set my team up in silence. I was concentrating so hard I blocked out everything else. Dale again checked my No.9 calling him dodgy and claiming that I couldn't use him. The others all agreed that I could use him as the tournament was well underway and that it was too late to object now.

I didn't respond and frankly, didn't care, I was just so fired-up and in the zone that I just simply carried on regardless. I also realised that having scraped a draw against Clint, if I could beat Dale now, it would more than likely put *The World Cup* beyond him.

Sedge had been pre-drawn to referee this match – which we both thought was unfortunate – Dale because Sedge and I were mates and he feared he would be biased towards me and me because I didn't think that Sedge had the experience to handle such a big game. So, after a couple of quick glugs of Stella to calm the nerves and 'pssk!' another can of beer opened followed by a few more glugs of beer the game started.

Dale kicked-off and the crowd was a 50-50 even split. Steve was cheering on Dale, Clint supporting me with Sedge playing the part of the impartial referee. And he was doing a very good job of it as well.

After a few minutes, Dale showing none of the edginess he displayed in his earlier game with Clint, cut through the middle and scored! One-nil. "Boyzees!!" came the familiar cry as he punched the air with delight. "Boyzees!" shouted Steve, grinning and patting him on the back. Not him as bloody well, I thought.

I set my team and kicked off. I immediately upped the pace of the game, running around the table for every flick, rushing and harrying Dale at every opportunity. I was putting him under constant pressure, shooting at every opportunity, no matter how desperate or vague the chance was, I kept him glued to his defensive duties and to his goal keeper. Then, halfway through the first half, my No.21 got the ball on the left-hand side of Dale's penalty area, took one touch and fired in a low, hard shot past his 'keeper! One - One. "Get in!" I shouted. Dale just gave a rueful smile and plucked the ball out of the back of his net.

He then re-set his men ready for the re-start. Steve was looking on more interestedly now. What he thought was going to be a tournament between just him and Dale was now going to be contested three ways. He could see that I was a force to be reckoned with!

Dale kicked-off and forced the ball into my scoring area. He flicked but missed the ball. My defender cleared the ball, it rolled down the right. My No.8 collected the ball and passed it into centre. My No.9 – my BIG No.9 – kicked the ball and it rolled into Dale's scoring area to the left. However, the player himself had spun away further left and had created too wide an angle to shoot from. The ball was a good five or six inches away from him and was too far to attempt a serious shot on goal so I had to flick him nearer. If I missed, Dale would surely clear the ball as he had a couple of defenders closing in on it.

I took careful aim, this would take a lot of skill. Too hard and I would accidentally kick the ball away from a scoring chance, too soft and I'd miss the ball completely. It had to be *just right*. I took aim, flicked my No.9 for his second kick (in Subbuteo, each player is allowed a maximum of 3 flicks before you have to use another player) I took aim and flicked... he slid forward – ooh it was going to be close, sooo close. He slid near the ball and started to slow down and just before he reached the ball, he stopped sliding! He teetered forward on his base – they are designed to spin and teeter and are weighted so that they stand back up again – and I think, being slightly taller than the normal Subbuteo player it helped as he leaned forward...

 forward... and then... 'tink'. You could just hear his head touch the ball. The touch was so light the ball barely moved and he rolled upright about an inch from the ball and facing the direction of the goal. Perfect! It was like a striker running onto his own pass,

controlling the ball with a deft nod of his head and without breaking stride he/I/both of us pounced on the shot and smacked it high into the roof of Dale's net! What a shot! What a goal!

"What a match!" cried Sedge. And it was. Two - One to me.

Dale was stunned. He just grinned nervously as he struggled to fish the ball out of the back of his net.

"Yessss!" I cried. "Two - one!" I was right in his face. After all the taunting and baiting he'd given me over the past few weeks, I was ready to ram it all down his throat!

After a frantic few minutes for both sides, the half-time bell rang. I was on fire! I was all over his defences and it was all he could do to fend me off. I was racing 'round the table, setting my men up for the second half, I couldn't wait for it to start. I took a couple more glugs of Stella, boy was this thirsty work! And I kicked off for the start of the second half.

I was still buzzing and playing at breakneck speed and Dale just couldn't keep up with me and was again on the back foot. I battered his defences again and again and eventually won a corner. I crossed the ball from the right to just inside the penalty area and again my big No.9 smashed the shot low and hard and into the left-hand side of the goal! Three - One!

"Yessss!" I cried. "Three - One!" I was winning. Finally, at last, I was winning. And not only was I winning but I was winning against Dale, against his beloved Peru, against his 'Boyzees!' And not only was I winning, I was thrashing him! I was dishing out a good and painful and long-overdue lesson to him and I was enjoying every-bloody-moment of it! I was Three - One up and there was daylight between us. If I crushed him underfoot, I'd only need to draw against Steve... In fact, because Dale had already dropped a point against Clint, I could still win the World Cup even if I lost to Steve and Dale beat him. If the remaining results went my way, I would be the World Champion...

I was in a spin! Or was I finally starting to feel the effects of all the Stella I'd been glugging? I don't know. But I was on cloud 9. And it was my No 9 who had put me there, and boy, was I ever going to enjoy this.

However, things rarely go to plan in the real world and like my earlier game against Chubby-Dodds at the tournament at his house, I did the unthinkable. I relaxed and let a two-goal lead slip away...

The realisation that I'd put three goals past Dale without reply and was smashing him easily made me take my foot off the pedal. Or perhaps, it was the relentless pace at which I'd been playing and just couldn't sustain the adrenaline. Certainly Dale couldn't keep up with it and I just started to run out of steam. I was hungry and thirsty and had drunk too much beer and was getting tired and I just... slowed down.

Dale, fighting for his 'Boyzees!' lives and to keep them in *The World Cup* came back at me with a vengeance. He turned the tables and all of a sudden it was me who was struggling to fend him off. He sliced through my defence and 'Bang!' Three - Two! That woke me up!

"Boyzees!" He cried, echoed by Steve. But this time, he didn't run round the table in victory, he quickly set his men ready for the re-start. There were three minutes left on the clock, plenty of time for more goals to be scored in a match like this!

I kicked off, desperately trying to take hold of the match again but he was having none of it. He kept the ball and it was him who was now playing with purpose and conviction. My flicks were off and I was even starting to miss the easiest of flicks. I was fading fast!

Sensing blood, the crowd was becoming more and more animated as Clint, Steve and even Sedge (who was still supposed to be refereeing) were all caught up in the excitement of Dale's comeback and me, clinging on for dear life!

Finally, with a minute-or-so to go, Dale cut though on his left-hand side, my right. He slipped the ball just inside a bit to get a better angle for himself and shot, low and hard past my flailing goalkeeper. "Boyzees!" came the familiar cry!

"Three – All!" announced Sedge.

Dale looked like a madman! He had a wild look in his eyes and looked like a man possessed with the thrill of the kill and his victim (me) in his sights.

We set for the kick-off, less than a minute to go. Would there be time for a winner?

I kicked off, ran the ball down to the right, moved into the middle, lined up for a shot but missed! His defender kicked it away but it hit another of my players. I pushed forward again, got into the shooting area, aimed and fired but his 'keeper was equal to it and the ball rolled on to one of his defenders. Then it was his turn to press. He cut through the middle, got into my shooting area, shot but my keeper saved it. The ball bounced off him and went for a corner kick. We quickly made our moves to position our men. He took the corner, the ball passed across to my right and he shot again. I missed it... Dale half-shouted "Boyz..." and Steve went to shout "Goal!" but it hit the post, rebounded back, hit my 'keeper on the back and went out for another corner on the other side! Clint, Sedge and me all shouted "Aaahhh!!!" or something similar and just at that moment, the bell rang for full time. Oh, the relief!

What a match! Just as Sedge had said earlier. What – a – match!

Exhausted and relieved, Dale and I immediately embraced each other in recognition of the fact that we had both just played the most exciting match of our lives and – I guess – it had the best possible outcome. A Three – All draw. It had goals, excitement and more thrills and near-misses than either of us had ever played before. And, more importantly than that, I had finally won Dale's respect as a player. I had pushed him all the way to the brink of defeat. He had to fight and claw and dig deep into his reserves to salvage a draw and keep himself in contention for title. If he thought he was going to win this competition the easy way, he was very much mistaken. I was going to rip that trophy out of his hands and there was no way he could stop me now!

Drained of both strength and emotion, I downed another can of lager. I had to slake my thirst in large gulps and to curb my growing hunger. I had used up so much energy in that one match I was exhausted! I had to sit down and have a breather.

Dale too was downing another can and grinning like a Cheshire cat. "Oh, boyzees... boyzees..." he mumbled "What a match..." shaking his head at his can of beer...

We were so exhausted, neither of us had the energy to get up and watch the next match. We just sat there grinning at each other from across the room, shaking our heads and drinking our beer. Even now, when I look back at this game, it was the most exciting match I'd ever played!

Result: Peru 3 – 3 Holland

The World Cup 1981
Standings after 5th Game

Teams	PLD	W	D	L	G/F	G/A	Diff	PTS
Uruguay	2	2	0	0	4	0	4	4
Holland	2	1	1	0	5	3	2	3
Peru	2	0	2	0	5	5	0	2
Belgium	2	0	1	1	2	4	-2	1
W Germany	2	0	0	2	0	4	-4	0

At this point, the league table showed the only thing that I was interested in; I was one full point ahead of Dale having played him. I only had to beat Clint — which I was confident of doing — and then, the big unknown... Steve and his Uruguay.

114

Chapter 9.
The big push!

Game 6. West Germany Vs. Belgium

Clint vs. Sedge. Belgium vs. West Germany.

The next match was always going to be an anti-climax after such an epic battle so perhaps it was fitting that it was contested between the two weakest players for the dreaded wooden spoon. Sedge, however, must have been learning fast from his previous games and watching how to play properly from ours because in this match he was certainly a different player to the one who'd been playing previously. He actually played very well and managed to hold Clint to Nil-Nil at half time. He'd even managed a shot or two of his own – which Clint had to save. But in the second half, Clint's patience was rewarded and Sedge conceded the only goal of the game.

Result: West Germany 0 – 1 Belgium

The World Cup 1981
Standings after 6th Game

Teams	PLD	W	D	L	G/F	G/A	Diff	PTS
Uruguay	2	2	0	0	4	0	4	4
Holland	2	1	1	0	5	3	2	3
Belgium	3	1	1	1	3	4	-1	3
Peru	2	0	2	0	5	5	0	2
W Germany	3	0	0	3	0	5	-5	0

Game 7. Peru Vs. Uruguay

Dale vs Steve. Peru Vs Uruguay.

Now I was _very_ interested to watch this match. I'd seen Steve play lesser opposition and put them away but this was to be his first real test of the evening. The pair knew each other's game well and were familiar adversaries. Dale had previously tried to tell us that Steve was equally as good, if not, the better player between them but really, he was just trying to unsettle us before the tournament. Make us think that we had no chance. Secretly, Dale believed himself to be top-dog.

I watched with eager anticipation and was pleased to see Steve playing well and he took an early lead. One – Nil!

This really did put Dale's back against the wall. He couldn't afford any more dropped points, he only had two from two games and Steve was potentially on six points. He had to win! So Dale dug deep and fought back, pushing Steve's Uruguayan defence back and back until eventually, just before half time, "Goal!" he cried. "Boyzees!" I don't know why I was surprised but he even said it to his mate. One – One at half time.

The second half resumed and I had done the calculation. If Steve held Dale to a draw, Dale certainly couldn't win the World Cup. It would come down to my game against Steve – with Dale watching helplessly on the side-lines.

However, there's *always* one thing you should NEVER do – especially when your *nemesis* is involved – and that's to count them out. Steve, as good as he was, wasn't able to contain Dale for the whole second half and Dale managed to squeeze a winning goal with just a couple of minutes left on the clock. Grinning but with a muted, yet slightly excited celebration he said "Boyzees!" and just bounced slightly as he realised he was going to win the game. Sadly for Steve, he just didn't have enough left in the tank to fight back and the game ended Two – One to Dale and this effectively killed-off Steve's chances of winning the tournament.

Result: Uruguay 1 – 2 Peru

The World Cup 1981
Standings after 7th Game

Teams	PLD	W	D	L	G/F	G/A	Diff	PTS
Uruguay	3	2	0	1	5	2	3	4
Peru	3	1	2	0	7	6	1	4
Holland	2	1	1	0	5	3	2	3
Belgium	3	1	1	1	3	4	- 1	3
W Germany	3	0	0	3	0	5	-5	0

This win put Dale level on points with Steve but with two more points almost certain to come his way as he only had Sedge left to play. I, on the other hand had a game in hand against Clint over both of them, so if I won my game, I would leap-frog them both. If Steve were to beat me, then he and Dale would be level on points and goal difference would count. If that was even, then it would be decided by their individual encounter – which Dale had won. So at this point, the highest I could see Steve finishing was second at best.

Therefore, the only person who could stop Dale now...was me.

Game 8. Belgium Vs. Holland

Ashley vs. Clint. Holland vs. Belgium.

Now I was looking forward to playing this game as I'd gotten over my initial nerves in my first match and was now rested after my titanic struggle with Dale in my second. Fortunately, I had been playing Clint regularly prior to this tournament in preparation and had the advantage of knowledge that Clint just couldn't beat me. I had always beaten him by three or four goals to nil. Occasionally he might score but he never really threatened to win a match and this one was to be no different. I cruised home a very comfortable winner by four goals to one. Not only did it put me on top of the pile by one clear point, I also had a superior goal difference to everyone else, and just like the first tournament, goal difference was going to play a major part in these finals.

Result: Holland 4 - 1 Belgium

The World Cup 1981
Standings after 8th Game

Teams	PLD	W	D	L	G/F	G/A	Diff	PTS
Holland	3	2	1	0	9	4	5	5
Uruguay	3	2	0	1	5	2	3	4
Peru	3	1	2	0	7	6	1	4
Belgium	4	1	1	2	4	8	- 4	3
W Germany	3	0	0	3	0	5	-5	0

I was in the driving seat with just two games left of the evening. I cracked open another can of beer, sat back and enjoyed watching Steve and Dale squirming in second and third place below me respectively. A draw would be a nice result. Victory would soon be mine...

Game 9. West Germany Vs. Peru

 But of course, as it always has been, drinking and driving is a sure-fire way to crash and burn and I had been drinking.

Game 9. Showed us the real Dale as he came out of the blocks firing on all cylinders and steam-rolled Sedge. Sedge was a mere novice compared to the master and Dale took full advantage of this. Now, Dale's goal difference at this point was +1 having scored seven but conceded six. Mine on the other hand was +5 having scored nine and conceded only four. Plus, I was a full point ahead of him and enjoying the position. So he realised that if he was to have any chance of keeping in touch with me he needed to have a big win to improve his position.

It's at this point – and I realise now whilst writing – that what makes someone a champion is their never-say-die attitude. The grit and determination that a true champion displays, in whatever field they may be in, is what _makes_ them a champion. For example, nowadays, in real football – at the original time of writing (2012)- Manchester United are the dominant force in the premier league, followed by Arsenal, Chelsea and now Manchester City. These few teams have contested the premiership title for the past ten years or so. But Manchester United have proven themselves to have been the most successful English side ever, even eclipsing Liverpool's long standing record of eighteen league titles. Now some people will say that United are a "lucky" team as they often manage to salvage a last-gasp goal to grab a point or come from behind to win a match when they haven't played particularly well, but they've managed to grind out a result. But the real truth is they are _not_ lucky. They've just worked bloody hard to be _better_ than their rivals. So when the game is in the 93rd minute (often referred to as '_Fergie-time_') with tired legs and battered bodies, United will often power through and score a goal because they are just that little bit fitter, little bit stronger and just that little bit more determined to grab a last gasp goal. No, it's certainly not luck.

Now Dale was very much the _Manchester United_ here for even though the title was effectively out of his hands, he played this game as though his life depended on it and he absolutely annihilated Sedge Seven – Nil! He was rampant. It was as though someone had made a recording of him shouting "Boyzees!" every two minutes as that was the rate at which the goals went in at. In fact, it seemed that the longest period of time without a goal was the time it took them to swap ends at half time.

After the fifth goal went in - and suitably shamed - Sedge just wanted to throw the towel in and stop playing. But Dale wouldn't let him, saying he had to finish the game, goal difference might count. Quite right too! But more than just spanking a far weaker player, what it did was this; It put Dale right back on top of the pile again, only this time, he was one point ahead of me and - more importantly - he had improved his goal difference. In fact, it was now better than mine. This meant, that in the final game of the night - me vs Steve - If I scored anything less than a win, it would hand the title straight to Dale! <u>HOW THE HELL DID THAT HAPPEN</u>??

I still can't believe this turn-a-round. Now the pressure was really on me.

Result: Peru 7 - 0 West Germany

The World Cup 1981
Standings after 9th Game

Teams	PLD	W	D	L	G/F	G/A	Diff	PTS
Peru	4	2	2	0	14	6	8	6
Holland	3	2	1	0	9	4	5	5
Uruguay	3	2	0	1	5	2	3	4
Belgium	4	1	1	2	4	8	- 4	3
W Germany	4	0	0	4	0	12	- 12	0

Game 10. Holland Vs. Uruguay

At last, the final game of the night. Ashley vs Steve. Holland vs Uruguay.

By now, it was getting late. Probably around 11:30, going on for mid-night. We had been playing for nearly four hours. And whilst it had been fun, I was getting very hungry and very, very tired. I also couldn't tell you how many cans of Stella I'd drunk in that time either. At least one per game and maybe another or two totted up in between. Perhaps five or six cans, I don't know. I was getting drunk! To be fair, we'd all been drinking so it was the same for all of us. However, Steve and Dale were seasoned drinkers and after five or six cans of beer they were only just starting to warm up. As for me, my head was starting to spin. We'd all thought to bring enough cans of beer but no-one thought to bring any food. I mean, we'd all eaten something before arriving but that was hours ago and what with all the excitement and adrenaline going through me I was absolutely famished. So by the time the final game started, I wasn't feeling very good.

I tried not to let this distract me but what with all that nervous energy having been spent, and the pressure of the last few games taking their toll on me I wasn't exactly in the right frame of mind to play. Thank god it was the last game.

So, we set up our teams ready for the kick-off. Now, it may just be how I'm remembering this or indeed that I wasn't feeling very well at this point but my vision started to go funny. To me, Steve's team just looked incredibly _dark._ I hadn't really noticed it before. The players had pale blue shirts on, but coupled with their black shorts, dark skin, black socks and black bases, they just looked so very dark.

Or perhaps it was the lighting. It was normal, living room lighting but it wasn't great. Whatever the reason, my eyes were straining. As I said, it was probably a combination of tiredness, being drunk, low sugar levels plus the fact that back then, almost everyone smoked and this was no exception. I couldn't see properly and was suddenly not in a good way.

Anyway, we kicked off and Dale was cheering and encouraging Steve whilst jeering me and generally trying to put me off my game. I didn't complain. As I said earlier, if you can't take it, don't dish it out. However, he needn't have bothered as I wasn't playing very well and Steve was. Eventually, mid-way through the first half, he scored. One - Nil "Boyzees!" he shouted.

"Boyzees!" shouted Dale – which was bloody irritating as I'd heard it enough times that evening without them both doing it.

I reset my men and kicked off, surviving until half-time without any further loss of goals. Fortunately, at this point, Clint's parents emerged to see what was happening – they'd been out for the evening and just popped their heads' in – Clint stated that we were in the middle of the final game and that things were very tense. As it stood, Dale would win *The World Cup*. Just as she was about to leave, Clint's mum said that there were some crisps and nibbles and soft drinks in the kitchen cupboard if anyone was hungry and would like some?

"Yes please!" I said and made Clint dash out and get me a bag of cheese and onion and some orange juice immediately! I'd practically swallowed the whole bag before I was ready to start the second half. Steve didn't seem to mind waiting as he was getting a 'pep' talk from Dale and tucking into his own bag of crisps.

So, partially, re-fuelled we started the second half and this time I was able to see clearly again, I wasn't tired and had caught my second wind. Most of the attacks came from me this time but try as I might, I just couldn't get the break I needed. He was very good defensively. However, with just a couple of minutes left to go, I upped the pace again, running around the table, applying more and more pressure, I finally managed to get into a good position for a clear shot and smacked the ball past his 'keeper and into the back of the net. One – One!

I was now back level on points with Dale so another goal would seal it for me, so I quickly re-set my men and pressed for the winner. We fought a tense battle to the end of the match and when the bell finally rang the score was still One – One. Not enough for me to have outright victory.

Bugger!

Result: Uruguay 1 – 1 Holland

The World Cup 1981
Standings after 10th Game

Teams	PLD	W	D	L	G/F	G/A	Diff	PTS
Peru	4	2	2	0	14	6	8	6
Holland	4	2	2	0	10	5	5	6
Uruguay	4	2	1	1	6	3	3	5
Belgium	4	1	1	2	4	8	- 4	3
W Germany	4	0	0	4	0	12	- 12	0

In fact, it was not enough for me to have victory at all.

Dale claimed he was World Champion due to the fact that he was top of the table on goal difference (+8 to my +5) plus, he'd scored more goals (14 to my 10). Either way, he was top of the league and not me. Owww!! How bloody unfair was that? Yet again, beaten by the smallest of margins *and* I hadn't even been beaten. Now the one scenario we didn't envisage at the beginning of the day and therefore didn't discuss it was "What if..." What if two or more teams finished level on points. Would there be a playoff? Would we have a World Cup Final or was it just going to be a straight league? We never imagined that after ten games of all-play-all that there would still be dead-lock. I argued until I was blue in the face that you couldn't win *The World Cup* on goal difference! There had to be an outright winner. But Dale was adamant. He was on top of the table and didn't care how you looked at it. He was on top in every way. Arrrggghh!! How frustrating!

However, after much discussion – and argument from me – it was agreed that the fairest thing to do was to play a decider. A final match, winner takes all. We would play a *World Cup Final*, to be decided by extra-time and penalties if so required.

So there we were, setting up, ready to go one more time!

Chapter 10.
The eleventh hour.

Game 11. Holland Vs. Peru

Now time was getting on. It was gone mid-night and we were all very much aware that we were probably outstaying our welcome at Clint's house but we had to have an outright winner. And although I had insisted on this final game, I was in no fit state to play it. I was hungry, thirsty, dry, tired, and - not to mention - just a little bit drunk! Dale of course, was far more seasoned. He was used to drinking and smoking heavily and playing in front of a crowd. After all, his "home pitch" was at the Bexley Working Man's club and often, he and Steve would play in front of a small group of on-lookers all watching whilst supping their pints.

The only one who was really fed-up was Steve. He hadn't won the tournament and he wasn't even second, not even close. After having a bright start against Sedge and Clint, his evening de-railed when Dale beat him and then he got even further pegged-back when he drew with me. So he was against us playing a final and just wanted to go home. However, as Dale was going to be driving him home, he had to wait. Sedge and Clint were tired too. Sedge was all Subbuteo'd-out and Clint was just well aware that it was late and his parents would want their house back so they could lock-up and go to bed.

The final thing I should point out at this juncture was that due to all of the above, we hadn't agreed to appoint a referee. A point that takes on greater significance and impact later on.

So there we were, all set, timer on, kick-off. Game on!

Well, any hopes of me repeating my earlier performance against Dale was just pure fantasy. I was awful. I was playing really badly from the start and to top it all, was starting to feel sick! All the beer, fags, smoke, and the hunger were all taking their toll. Back then, we all smoked, and although I was never a heavy smoker, I'd probably had more than I was used to, and on top of everything else, I was feeling quite unwell.

Anyway, Dale – who had had the benefit of a break after his easy game against Sedge, was certainly more refreshed than I was and soon scored. "Boyzees! One - nil!" he cried.

Damn!

We set up and I kicked-off. Dale was determined to win this match and pressed for a second. Under this onslaught, my defence gave way and he scored again! Two - Nil.

"Boyzees!" This time it was with a little more gusto.

I was not feeling good.

However, I made it to half-time without any further loss. I grabbed some crisps, had another glug of orange juice and nipped to the loo to buy some time. I splashed water on my face and tried to wake up! Then I gave myself a stiff-talking to in the mirror and pulled myself together.

It worked! The second half started better for me and I was forcing Dale further and further back into his own half but he was defending very well. I was playing solidly but just not getting the break I needed. To make matters worse, I carelessly gave away possession in Dale's half and he advanced through the middle. His player pushed forward and both he and the ball were just inside my penalty area when he flicked his player and _just_ missed the ball. It was my turn to flick but I didn't really have a defender in a good enough position to make a confident clearance. If I missed, Dale was ready to pounce and shoot for goal. I took careful aim, flicked and... My player simultaneously hit both his player and the ball! It was almost at the same time... but not quite...

It was a foul. A penalty...

"Penalty!" shouted Dale.

... or, at least it should have been.

"No!" I shouted. "It hit at the same time!" I said.

At this, the others edged closer to the table. They hadn't really been watching – they were all getting tired and fed-up as well.

"Didn't see it" said Clint.

Steve and Sedge didn't say anything.

"It's a penalty!" Said Dale "Who's refereeing anyway?"

"It's not!" I said "it hit at the same time!" I felt really bad. I was cheating, being dishonest, and that really wasn't me – or so I thought – but I was desperate! I really wanted to stay in the match. If he scored a penalty, that would be it, and I was so desperate not to lose. Not to him. Not again.

I also wanted a bit of equality from the two-legged match. I'd been fair - or generous - then when I'd let him play the advantage and he went on to score. This was just/almost/nearly as border line as that. He should be fair to me and let me have the benefit of the doubt... But no, he was standing his ground.

"It's a Penalty!"

"No! It's not! " I cried. "You're two-nil up already" I argued, like that was any reason not to give it.

Dale looked really pissed-off! Rightly so. I was cheating.

"Alright then," said Dale "but I _know_ it was a penalty!"

We played on and I cleared the ball. Dale was clearly put off by my poor sportsmanship and lost some of his enthusiasm for the match.

I carried on, desperately trying to get back into the match but time was ebbing away. However, with less than a couple of minutes left on the clock, I scored. Realising that I'd probably soured the match by not owning up to the penalty, I didn't celebrate the goal and just set my men up.

"Oh God! Don't bloody-well equalise," Said Steve, "I want to go home!"

There was no fear of that happening. Dale snapped out of his malaise and played extremely well for the last couple of minutes and as it got nearer and nearer the end, his mood lightened and he was starting to commentate on his own flicks.

"Boyzee up the middle, to Boyzee... great pass! Boyzee flicks across from the wing to Boyzee..." He was starting to enjoy himself again as the seconds ticked down. It was all I could do to stand and watch him as the seconds ticked down.

Finally, the bell went and put us all out of our misery. Dale had won Two - One fair and square and was the World champion. I couldn't argue. Not only had he topped the league but he had won the Final as well!

World Cup Final

Peru 2 - 1 Holland

Dale was buoyant again, celebrating and chanting "Boyzees! Boyzees! Boyzees!"

Dale hoisted the small trophy above his head and did a little jig! Then he placed all his players around it in the middle of the pitch, chanting "Boyzees! Boyzees! Boyzees!"

Steve just grabbed his coat and said "Come on Dale, let's go!"

Sedge got his coat and I packed my teams. Clint was almost asleep but managed to tell Dale to keep the noise down as his parents had gone to bed.

I put on my coat, congratulated Dale, said thanks to Clint for hosting the evening and went out to the car with Sedge who drove me home.

Still feeling a little unwell I sat there in silence for most of the journey back home. Eventually, I said to Sedge "it *was* a penalty you know".

"Yes," he said "I saw".

"And you didn't say anything?"

"No point. I could see he was going to win anyway, he didn't need the penalty. I could see you were flagging".

Now, I'd like to say, in defence of my actions that very nearly ruined an otherwise truly great, fun evening, is that I'm not a cheat. Well, not *usually*. It's just that on _this_ occasion when everything leading up to it had been filled with near misses and taunting and teasing and frustration and knowing the merciless ribbing I was going to get on Monday at work - from both Dale and everyone else - well, it was just too much to bear. I was desperate.

If I was going to lose, it _had_ to be close. Not thrashed three or four nil! But you know what? In hindsight, maybe I should have been and kept my dignity. Or at least, left it as it was, with Dale winning on goal-difference and me remaining unbeaten. After all, he couldn't really have had bragging rights if he hadn't _beaten_ me could he? Not if he'd only won on 'goal-difference'. I could have still claimed he wasn't better than me if he hadn't beaten me... but he had. And what's worse is I'd insisted upon it... and I'd cheated.

I didn't sleep well that night.

Chapter 11.
'Cheat!'

Back in work on Monday, word had got around that Dale had won *The World Cup*.

Unusually for me, on this occasion, I was in work before Dale and was greeted with a few jokes and jeers from T-Dubs, Eva, Sherlock, Chubby et-al.

Finally, Dale walked in – or should I say, bounced in – Boyzees in one hand, the World Cup trophy in the other and a huge grin on his smug, punchable face!

He placed both the World Cup and his Boyzees on his desk facing me, and then regaled tales of the Friday night. How he'd 'tonked' Sedge, drawn a close, tense match with Clint, came from behind to beat his mate Steve and then... beaten me in the final. He told everyone how I'd *cheated* over the penalty incident but had still lost! There was no mention of our fantastic, earlier game where I'd so very nearly beaten him and had won his respect. Nothing at all. It was awful.

The only player Dale had any respect for was Clint.

"Clint at least held me to a draw." he crowed "And he's the only one out of all of you – Chubby included - that I haven't yet beaten. So by virtue of that, I'm the champ, then its Clint, then the also-rans' (Chubby & Sedge) and then the cheats!" (Three guesses who he means here.)

"And as such, we should be treated with respect as befitting the best and second best Subbuteo players in the company. So Dunny-boy...get your fags out!"

How bloody irritating!

On top of this, I had T-Dubs walking past at every opportunity shouting "Penalty!" or asking "Was it Two - Nil or Three - Nil?"

And I would have to correct him "No Trev, it was Two - One".

"Oh yes..." he'd say, "that's because you *cheated* isn't it?..." and everybody laughed.

Sigh.

Who said it was only a game?

Chapter 12.
The Tonking Of
Turkington!

All through that summer, Subbuteo was high on the list of activities. We all played more frequently. Me, mainly because I have an obsessive nature about things I'm interested in and wanted – nay needed – to practice. And also because it was fun. We all enjoyed the boyish charm this simple game gave to us and of course, the bragging rights that went with it. To the victor the spoils!

I, of course, avoided playing Dale like the plague as I wanted to be sure I could beat him when eventually we did play. I couldn't risk another defeat at his hands, so I went on playing Clint, Sedge, Laurence and Chubby, beating them all with relative ease.

One of the games I enjoyed most was against Chubby at my house. I decided that I needed some stiffer opposition to the usual fare I was getting and asked him round for a match at mine. Plus, I was still slightly irritated with myself for letting a two-goal lead slip when I'd last played him at his house and was determined to put that right. So I challenged him to a return match - not a two-legged match you understand - but a *return* match after the two-all draw at his. And this time I was *determined* to punish him, and win the match convincingly.

He was very pleased to have been asked, and to my surprise, he turned up! I thought he might have pulled out as he had done in the past but he didn't. He also brought his favourite team, Sweden.

Out of respect for him coming over, I treated him to the full works of my collection. I set the pitch up, complete with floodlights, scoreboards, ball-boys, throw-in figures, the referee, linesmen, timer and crowd barriers with advertising billboards stuck to them. I even displayed my European Cup trophy, although I made it clear that we were <u>not</u> playing for that! I also got out my ball-raising chute for

corners. Chubby was comfortable with this accessory as he had one and knew how to use it and agreed we could use it in the match. One final touch - which Chubby appreciated - was 'the crowd'. I had set up every single one of my Subbuteo teams either side of the goals to represent the crowd, cheering on the match. All the players I had were on display. Chubby loved it.

"I'm gonna do that with all my teams!" he roared. He was an even bigger kid than I was.

So, we set up. I was playing Chile. Ever since the World Cup using Holland, I decided the only way to go was to use *my team* at every available opportunity. Win, lose or draw I would do it with Chile.

Chubby set up with his favourite team Sweden and we were ready. I won the toss and so chose to kick-off. I had been planning my strategy for this match for a while and everything was going according to plan. In my previous games with Chubby, Dale or Clint, I always found that I was far more successful if I played at a very fast pace, passing quickly and running around the table and shooting at every opportunity. This had the effect of keeping your opponent on the back-foot, and as you didn't have to wait for them to be ready with their goal-keeper it meant that they always had to be cautious when attacking themselves for as soon as they would lose possession, I was on top of them. This tactic usually worked for me and in fact, when I'd played like this, no-one had been able to resist my attacks for long – not even Dale. The only downside to this though was it was extremely difficult to maintain throughout a whole match. I would simply run out of steam eventually and then my opponents could fight back and I'd get caught myself. This led to the games being very high-scoring, open affairs, just like that great game with Dale in the World Cup. Going One – Nil down, Three – One up, then clinging on for dear life at Three – Three! Great fun for the spectators but terribly stressful for the players.

So, leading up to this match, I'd been putting in some extra training to build up my stamina so as not to run out of steam and practiced as much as I could, playing at breakneck speed around my table. It was not so much the overall fitness I had to try and maintain it was the adrenalin rush from the competition that was hard to reproduce in practice.

Anyway, it wasn't long before I'd caught Chubby cold with a goal and went One – Nil up. He looked stunned and tried valiantly to fight back but before long, I was sprinting around the table and 'bang!' Two – Nil!

Unfortunately, however, with a couple of minutes to go before half time, I started to slow down and he managed to claw his way back into the game. A swift break down the right, he passed the ball over to the middle, took careful aim and slotted the ball perfectly past my 'keeper.

"Whoaaa!!! Turkington!!!" He cried! I'd almost forgotten his goal celebration and he clenched his teeth and ran up to me waving his fists in the air shouting "Come on!!" right in my face and growling "Game on!". I honestly thought he was going to punch me!

Clearly, he had learned nothing as his protracted goal celebrations meant that he was wasting his own time and we finished the first half at Two - One to me.

In the second half, I resumed my attacking flow and managed to win an early corner. I made my flicks to position my men all on the edge of the goal-keeper's six-yard box and waited for him to take his three flicks to place defenders to mark my men. Just as I'd planned, he fell into my trap and had  flicked his men to mark mine making the edge of the six-yard box a heaving mass of forwards and defenders. I placed the ball-raising chute on the corner triangle, selected my corner-kicker and flicked the ball. Now I had done this very thing, many, many times in my own practice games so knew exactly what to expect when I flicked. The ball floated high above the pitch and dropped down on top of the heaving throng of players just as I'd planned. The ball _could_ have gone anywhere when it landed but it didn't. It landed right on top of one of the players (defender or forward it didn't really matter which) and it spun off into the goal past Chubby's flailing 'keeper.

"What a goal!" I cried!

"How the hell did you manage that?" said Chubby.

"You fell into my trap and helped me pack out the goal mouth with your players as well as mine, gave me a larger target to aim for".

Three – one.

Irritated with himself that he had fallen for my tactic, Chubby came surging back at me with renewed vigour. After pressing a little too much though, he left himself exposed at the back to a counter-attack and I broke through again. Bang!

Four – One!

Again, Chubby came at me and I had to defend resolutely. However, respect where it's due, Chubby was no slouch at Subbuteo and he could play quite well himself at times and he kept plugging away. Eventually, his patience was rewarded and he managed to score a second goal.

Four – Two!

This time however, he just gave a muted, aggressive "Come on!" to himself and re-set his men.

But time was running short and I kept taking the attack to him. My tactics were paying-off and I was confident that although he could score, I knew that I too could also score and was happy with that "If you score one, I'll score two" mentality.

Finally, the bell rang and the game ended at Four – Two to me.

After the match, we chatted briefly but he was clearly irritated at having lost the match. I asked if he'd like another game but, still being irritated at having lost the first match – especially as it wasn't even that close – he made his excuses and left.

At work the following day, Dale enquired about our game and before I could say anything, Chubby came rushing over to give his version of the match, which basically consisted of him "running" the match, scoring two brilliant goals and me catching him on the break and scoring (four) lucky goals.

"Did he cheat?" asked Dale.

Sigh.

I of course, ignored his comment and countered that it was my brilliance that won me the game and I regaled tales of how I'd scored the best goal of the evening with a "wonderful header" from a set piece using the ball-raising chute. It was great fun!

A cartoon clipping Dale gave
me when I left the company

Chapter 13.
All is revealed!

One evening after work, we all went down the pub to celebrate T-Dubs birthday. There had been plenty of drunken banter between us all and of course the conversation came around to Subbuteo. Dale was being his usual boorish self, claiming that he was unbeatable and by far the best player he knew. Modesty was obviously *not* his strongest point.

"I'm just too good for you Boyzee" he'd say, whilst blowing the smoke from his Marlboro cigarette into my face...

"You know I'm right. I haven't lost a single game since we started... and don't go on about that 'two-legged' match again. You lost. I won!"

The pub was packed full of people from the local offices and we were huddled together in our little group, T-dubs, Chubby, Sherlock, Dale, Clint, Sedge and me when the door opened and in walked some of the girls from the office. As it was his birthday, tradition meant that T-Dubs was 'in the chair' and bought them all a drink. The conversation then turned to birthdays and star-signs. I knew Sedge was a Capricorn as he shared his birthday with Elvis

Presley, January the 8th "Another 'King', Dunny-boy" he would say. I happened to mention that I was a Piscean when Dale looked at me and smiled and said "Oh really? Me too!" We looked at each other for a moment and then without warning started to play 'guess the birthday!'

He said, "Is it in March or February?"

"March!"

"Me too!" he said, getting excited.

Then I said, "Is it near the beginning or near the middle?"

"Nearer the beginning"

"Me too!" getting even more excited.

"Is it in single or double figures?"

"Single" I said. The suspense was mounting.

"Me too!" exclaimed Dale. "Look! Let's just say it, after three. One, two, three..."

"Ninth!" We both shouted at the same time.

Bugger me! You could have knocked me down with a feather.

"Oh my God," said Sedge, "You two have the same birthday! Oh my God."

Dale was just as wide-eyed and as speechless as I was.

The fact that he was older than me and thereby had the birthday first didn't matter to me. It was _my_ birthday, not his! There are three hundred and sixty-four other bleedin' days of the year he could have had. Three hundred and sixty-five if you count a leap year but _OH NO_, he has to go and have _MY_ birthday as well. Doesn't that just about explain everything? I'd been competing against myself. And what's more, I was losing!

Just then, squeezing herself through the crowd to come and join us was Janice. She slipped between Clint and Sherlock and as she did, Sedge leaned across - non-too-subtly - in front of Jo to have a look at her derrière as she passed. He looked at T-Dubs, puffed out his cheeks and mouthed "_Phwoar!_" with a big grin on his face. T-Dubs just gave a slight nod and smiled back, suppressing the urge to laugh. Finally, Janice stopped moving and stood next to T-Dubs. He barely moved but she leaned in close to his ear and said in a voice loud enough for us to hear, "I'm just picking something up for dinner then I'll be straight home. Don't be too late... not if you want your present..." Then she pecked him on the cheek, turned to us and with a big beautiful grin, said "Night boys!" and she waltzed out of the pub.

We all stood there open-mouthed. No-body said a word. Least of all Sedge who was now turning an incredible beetroot colour because he'd just been caught red-handed ogling Janice's backside! T-Dubs just stood there staring straight ahead with his pint in his hand. Eventually, he sniffed, lifted his pint, cracked a little smile, took a very large swig of his pint then said, "Right boys! Time for one more, then I'm off home. It appears I'm on a promise!"

Once again, you could have knocked us down with a feather.

Even Dale was gob-smacked.

"You old dog Trevor! How long has that been going on?"

"Oh, you know, Thorners..." said T-Dubs "You've either got it or you haven't...and it looks like I've got it! Ha, ha, ha!"

The next day at work, both T-Dubs and Janice were in fine form, laughing, joking and flirting openly with each other. Janice was again wearing her tight lilac sweater. Just as she was leaving she turned to Sedge and purred "I put this on for you today Paul, I hear you like it?" Then she flashed him a gorgeous smile and wiggled off down the corridor!

Sedge went bright beetroot red again and cowered down. T-Dubs shouted across the office "Is it me or is it getting hot in here? I'd better open a window. I can feel the heat from over here! Ha, ha, ha!"

Poor old Sedge just slid forward in his chair and hid his face on his desk in embarrassment. Suitably shamed, it was my turn to say "Come on, Seggie - boy... get 'em aht!" and he had to dish his fags out.

Everyone was laughing.

West Germany

Chapter 14.
World War Two!

It was later on that summer – and many more games later - that the suggestion was made to hold another World Cup.

The suggestion probably came from me as I couldn't bear the thought that Dale was still the champion and yet I was beating everyone else I played. Dale to his credit was sporting enough to agree and put his title on the line – although he did say he thought the world cup winner should hold the title for four years but that wasn't really practical – so we agreed that we would hold it at four-month intervals. The football being played was in miniature so it stood to reason that the timeline should be scaled down too.

Clint was reluctant to hold it at his house again as it had gone on rather late last time and didn't think his parents would be too happy with it. Besides, as with the real world cup, there is always a different host every time it was staged so it was only fair that this would be no different.

I was the obvious candidate as Chubby had held an evening at his, so had Clint. Sedge didn't have any of the equipment what-so-ever so he couldn't hold it unless we lent him the stuff but... *Subbuteo is so precious*... Plus, it wouldn't feel like you were playing an away match if you were still playing on your own pitch! And as for Dale, well, nobody could agree to going to his social club as it was so far away (relatively speaking) from the rest of us and only Sedge had a car. Plus, Dale couldn't guarantee us having access to the club's games table on which we'd lay the pitch for the entire evening without first clearing it with the club in case they wanted to use it. The table was situated in a quieter part of the club, apparently usually reserved for playing cards, cribbage or dominoes and our raucous behaviour may upset a few of the old codgers.

So there it was, the World Cup # 2 would be held at my house.

This time, I asked my brother Laurence if he would be interested in joining in the fun and he was very keen. The more, the merrier I thought. That meant that we would have Me, Dale, Laurence, Steve, Chubby, Sedge and Clint. Wow! Seven of us all competing. Fantastic! It would be like more World War Two.

We agreed that we couldn't play an all-play-all tournament as before as that would take too long to get through, however, we could play two groups then a knockout phase like the real world cup. We could even have seedings and draw lots. Dale and I would be numbered one and two of course and like the real tournament be separated at the group stage. Then we would draw the rest of the players into the two groups. Three in one, four in the other (unless someone either dropped-in or out) and it would revert to an even number in each group. We also decided that the top two teams from each group would qualify for the *semi-final*. The winner of group A would play the runner-up of group B and the winner of group B would play the runner-up of group A. This would practically ensure that both Dale and I would qualify for the semis and – barring accidents – most likely play in the final, unless Steve or Laurence or Chubby got extremely lucky.

However, as soon as it was announced and organised, Chubby bailed-out with yet another lame excuse. I realised immediately, that he just couldn't bear to take part and risk losing more than one game. His temperament wouldn't allow it. He just couldn't bear the thought of knowing that I could beat him, Dale could beat him, Steve (most probably) could beat him, and now, along with my brother participating and Clint's new-found status as "the number Two best player" (according to Dale) that even *he* would be threatening to beat him. No. That was too much for him to take and he chickened out.

Surprisingly, even Steve pulled out. According to Dale, he was going to be working late that night and wouldn't be able to come. Now I have my doubts, I think it was for the same reason as Chubby. He only came third last time and I think he was scared of finishing even lower.

Then, to cap it all, Sedge decided to drop out as well. But at least he was honest about it. He said he didn't want to be thrashed by Dale and myself again either and didn't want to suffer the humiliation of coming last and probably not even scoring. He'd rather go round to Debs' and score there! It was a real shame. It would have been great to have had everyone participating as I'd planned but rather than wait and try and convince everyone to get back on-board and re-arrange another time to play, I was too impatient. I couldn't just sit back and wait for everyone to change their minds. I wanted to play. Perhaps if I'd been the champion, then maybe that would have been different. I wouldn't have been in such a hurry to risk my championship status. But I desperately wanted to beat Dale and become champion myself. I thought they could join in on the next one – _if_ we ever played another tournament – and if not, well, then, I'd have to retire as champion... Or so I'd hoped.

So with this turn of events it just left the four of us competing. Me, Dale, Clint and

Laurence. Not much of a turnout for a world
cup I thought.

England

Chapter 15.
It all kicks off!

So there it was, World Cup #2 was going to be contested between Me, Dale, Clint and Laurence and due to the lack of numbers competing, it was agreed that we'd play an all-play-all league format (as before) but on this occasion Dale insisted that the team who finished on top - even if it was just on goal difference - would be the winner! There would be no replay or final as before. You had to win the group to win *the world cup*.

I didn't particularly like this way of deciding the tournament but both Laurence and Clint agreed and so I was out-voted. In hindsight, I actually didn't like the thought that I could win the group on goal difference only to lose to Dale in the final. If we'd had the other guys playing as well, then for sure, top two go through and you then risk it in the knock-out phase but this was just a one shot only chance. No pressure then!

The order of play was decided and the first match was to be Dale vs Clint. Peru vs Belgium. A re-match of the opening game of the first world cup where Clint's humble Belgium stunned Dale's '*Boyzees*!' into a thrilling Two

- Two draw. Could yet another shock be on the cards?

Game 1. Belgium Vs. Peru

No, actually. Dale showed no signs what-so-ever of being nervous in this match. Perhaps because he wasn't getting the barracking he was getting in their first encounter but he played steadily and  calmly and blocked out all of Nigel's attempts on goal. By half-time, Dale was one - nil up. At the end of the match it was Two - Nil. First blood to Dale!

Result: Peru 2 - 0 Belgium

The 2nd World Cup 1981
Standings after 1st Game

Teams	PLD	W	D	L	G/F	G/A	Diff	PTS
Peru	1	1	0	0	2	0	2	2
Chile	0	0	0	0	0	0	0	0
England	0	0	0	0	0	0	0	0
Belgium	1	0	0	1	0	2	-2	0

Game 2. England Vs. Chile

This should have been a relatively comfortable match for me, playing against Laurence as I had been all that summer. I didn't recall a single loss to him. The match started  straightforward enough but it was very soon obvious that he wanted to win and he proved to be a very difficult nut to crack! By half-time I was already struggling and we changed ends with the score at One – One. However, half-way through the second half, I was advancing down the left wing, had just flicked the ball into his scoring area when... brrrp, brrrp... brrrp, brrrp... The phone rang! Back then in the '70's and '80's we had a very natty little landline phone called a *Trim phone* which had a very distinctive ring, unlike the more common *'ring, ring'* type of phones people used to have. This was a very high-pitched, trill kind of sound and it was putting me off! I looked at Laurence, he looked at me. The phone was ringing just outside the door – because back then, the phone was usually situated in the hall at the bottom of the stairs – and we knew one of us should answer it. But neither of us moved or wanted to leave the match at such a crucial point, especially as the clock was ticking away and vital seconds were being lost! Suddenly, it stopped and my mum shouted "Ash! It's Helen!"

Thankfully, mother had answered the phone and it was my then girlfriend 'Helen'. I shot Laurence a pleading look and he said "Ok, stop the clock."

"Thanks" I said and ran to the phone. "What's up?" I said.

"Nothing" She replied. "I just wanted to see how you're getting on?"

Now, I know it was nice of her to ring, but... Don't you women get it? You don't ring someone in the middle of a footy tournament to ask "how it's going?" My god! I was almost speechless as I gasped "You... you're asking me *this*? *Now*?... Couldn't you wait till I rang *you*?"

She wasn't happy, "Fine! I was only asking! I shouldn't have bothered!" Slam! Down went the receiver her end.

I stood there briefly, should I ring back and apologise or should I get back to the match? I *should* ring, I thought... but then I ran back to the match! Laurence was waiting (and Dale and Clint as well) and the clock had been stopped for me. I couldn't hold them all up at such a crucial point in the game. I ran back to the table, apologised to them all, muttering something about "Bloody women! Don't they know not to interrupt the footy..." I glanced briefly at Dale who had that smug grin on his face again, knowing that I had just been given grief by Helen and that it might just serve to put me off. I tried to ignore him and re-positioned myself ready to take my shot. Dale re-started the clock and I asked Laurence if he was ready, he acquiesced. I took careful aim with my No. 10 and flicked a beautiful shot past Laurence's 'keeper into the back of the net! Two – one! And to be fair to him, he didn't complain about the interruption.

Laurence fought back bravely but fortunately, I managed to hold him off until the final bell rang. Dale of course, being the mischievous little git he could be, was trying to stir things up by saying that my goal shouldn't have stood as I had run away from the table during the game to answer the phone. He was suggesting that I should forfeit the match or at least, replay it. Laurence, however, was being a little more magnanimous about it and let the result stand.

Result: England 1 – 2 Chile

Teams	PLD	W	D	L	G/F	G/A	Diff	PTS
Peru	1	1	0	0	2	0	2	2
Chile	1	1	0	0	2	1	1	2
England	1	0	0	1	1	2	-1	0
Belgium	1	0	0	1	0	2	-2	0

Immediately after the match I dashed to the phone and rang Helen back to apologise. However, her mother answered and told me that she had apparently "gone out" and didn't know what time she would be back. I left a grovelling apology with her mother and said that I would call her tomorrow.

Game 3. Belgium Vs. Chile

As there were only four of us competing, it meant that on occasion, someone would have to play two games in a row. This time it was me. I was playing Clint.

However, as I was setting my men up to play the match, the phone rang again! I looked at Laurence and he looked at me. I said "Sorry

Clint, I'll just be a sec." And I ran to the phone. It was Helen. "I thought you'd gone out?" I said.

"Well, I told my mum to say that because I was annoyed with you but she said you sounded sorry so I thought I'd give you a call back and say 'sorry' too." She cooed.

"Ah, well, thing is, I'm just setting up for the next game..."

"You mean you're not going to stay and talk to me now that I've forgiven your rude behaviour and now you're going off again?" she said.

"Well, we're in the middle of..."

"Oh go on then! Go back to your little kids game!" Slam went the receiver again. I briefly wondered how robust her phone must be if it kept getting slammed down like that.

"Ash? Are you coming?" shouted Laurence. "Nigel's ready to kick-off."

"He's not the only one." I muttered as I entered the room and resumed setting up my men.

As I set my men, Dale was standing the other side of the table grinning at me like a Cheshire cat, giving me his 'I know you've just been given a hard time, look' and was obviously hoping my phone call would put me off. However, that 'look' from Dale made me more determined than ever!

Fortunately for me, I'd had lots of practice against Clint, having spanked him throughout the summer, so I was in confident mood to get a good score against him. "Rack up some goal difference" I thought, which is exactly what I managed to do. Clint put up scant resistance and I trotted-out a comfortable Four – Nil winner. This made my goal difference look quite impressive and put me on top of the group with one game left to play.

"That shut you up, you smug git!" I said to Dale.

Result: Chile 4 – 0 Belgium

The 2nd World Cup 1981
Standings after 3rd Game

Teams	PLD	W	D	L	G/F	G/A	Diff	PTS
Chile	2	2	0	0	6	1	5	4
Peru	1	1	0	0	2	0	2	2
England	1	0	0	1	1	2	-1	0
Belgium	2	0	0	2	0	6	-6	0

Chapter 16.
Anything you can do...

Game 4. England Vs. Peru

Game four was between Laurence and Dale and having had such a tough time getting past Laurence myself, I was hopeful that he would give Dale just as tough a game as he had given me.  I was also confident that given my reasonably impressive goal difference, that even if he lost, it would still put me firmly in the driving seat. As long as it was close...

So when the bell rang at half-time with the score One - Nil to Dale, I was reasonably happy. If he managed to win two or even three nil, that would still be ok. After all, this was Laurence he was playing, not Sedge...

However, underestimate your enemies at your peril! And that is exactly what I did with Dale.

In the second half, Dale gave Laurence a lesson in playing Subbuteo and when his fourth goal went in with a few minutes still left on the clock, I couldn't help myself but to shout an irritated "Laurence!" at my brother.

"I'm not losing on purpose!" He cried. But I was just _so_ irritated! My goal difference had gone and now it was Dale who was back in the driving seat. Dale, of course, was as smug-as-ever with that bloody, big grin of his and bouncing round the table as he continued to enjoy himself. Shortly before the bell rang, his familiar cry of "Boyzees!" rang out for a fifth, irritating, time. Laurence had been thrashed FIVE – NIL! It might just as well have been Sedge he played.

Why, oh why, does it always fall to me to beat him? Why can't someone else at least put up the slightest bit of resistance? Why? They _always_ roll over when they play the 'big-boy' but when it's me, they fight as though their bloody lives depended on it! Why is that? Why do I have to fight the whole bloody way and the other guy gets it easy? Why? Why? _WHY?_

At least, that's how it seemed to me anyway.

Dale's romp over Laurence meant that he was now comfortably on top and I had the mountain to climb. I had to go all out for a win. A draw now would be no good to me what-so-ever.

Result: Peru 5 - 0 England

The 2nd World Cup 1981
Standings after 4th Game

Teams	PLD	W	D	L	G/F	G/A	Diff	PTS
Peru	2	2	0	0	7	0	7	4
Chile	2	2	0	0	6	1	5	4
England	2	0	0	2	1	7	-6	0
Belgium	2	0	0	2	0	6	-6	0

Game 5. England Vs. Belgium

However, before that match could happen, we had to play for the wooden spoon. Both Laurence and Nigel had lost their first two matches and both were eager to avoid a third, hence getting white-washed.

Laurence however, fresh from his thrashing at the hands of Dale had clearly picked up a few pointers on how to play the

damned game and romped home a comfortable Three
- Nil winner. He was pleased but it was too
little, too late as far as I was concerned.

Result: Belgium 0 - 3 England

The 2nd World Cup 1981
Standings after 5th Game

Teams	PLD	W	D	L	G/F	G/A	Diff	PTS
Peru	2	2	0	0	7	0	7	4
Chile	2	2	0	0	6	1	5	4
England	3	1	0	2	4	7	-3	2
Belgium	3	0	0	3	0	9	-9	0

After a short break and a couple of swigs
of beer (I was being very careful this time
not to have too much!) Dale and I set our teams
up. Although this was not quite a *final* it
would act like one. It was the last game of
the night. We were both on top of the group,
separated by the dreaded goal difference once
again.

I didn't care though at this point. I
knew, I think I always *knew* that it would come
to this. I would have to beat him to win the
trophy, to be champion. It was only right, he

was the champion and I was the challenger. In boxing, in the event of a draw, the champion retains his title. Same as in Chess. To be the champ you had to BEAT the champ. This was no different.

And this time, I was going to beat him!

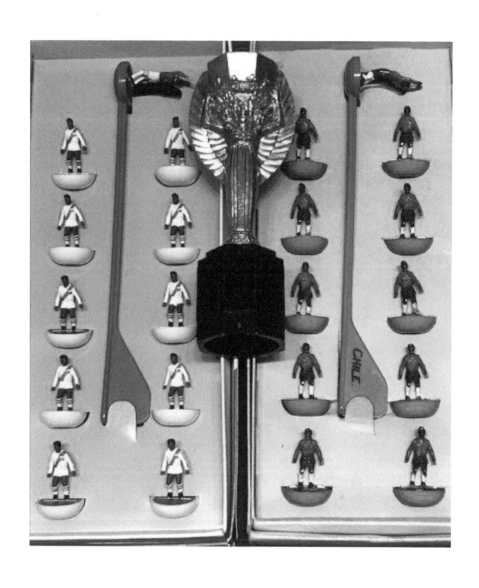

Peru vs. Chile

For the World Cup Trophy

Chapter 17.
Mt. Olympus awaits.

Game 6. Chile Vs. Peru

Dale won the toss and kicked-off. By now, I had seen him play enough times to know how he liked to set his men and how he liked to start so I revised my formation accordingly and managed to negate his  attacking strategy. Dale was a very fluid player and quite skilled in making these little men swerve and move around the pitch. What made it all the more exciting was that I could match him flick-for-flick. And just like all our previous matches this one was as tight as tight could be!

At half-time, the score was nil – nil. We changed ends and Laurence set the timer. I kicked-off and the hostilities resumed, cut and thrust, advance and fall-back, the match was end-to-end stuff. I was running around the table like a man possessed and Dale, to his credit, was defending heroically.

The game was *so* tense and *so* tight neither of us paid any attention to the clock. It was as if you were watching a dangerous animal. If either of you took your eyes off the other you were done for, such was the intensity that this game was played.

Anyway, Dale had just pushed the ball down to my left, flicked and then missed it. I took my flick and curled my mid-fielder – my No. 7 – around the ball and passed it forward. It rolled to just outside Dale's scoring area. I carefully advanced down the left-hand side, the ball pushed just into the scoring area by my captain the No. 11. He was perfectly placed behind the ball. Then, suddenly, we heard it! A small tinny 'tink' sound. Now, what I haven't mentioned before is that Subbuteo used to sell 'game timers' as part of their accessories range. The truth was, these were just standard egg timers that had a large dial that you twisted to the required time and it would tick

away rather loudly. They were none-too-accurate with their time-keeping either as it was of the coiled-spring variety type of clock and could only be *roughly* set.

It also had a very mechanical 'ticka-ticka-ticka' sound to it and you could almost imagine the innards rocking so hard back-and-forth as it counted the seconds down that if it didn't have such a good solid base, it would have rocked itself over! Still, it was better than nothing and we all played by the ring of the bell.

Anyway, this game timer, _my_ game timer had another peculiar quirk about it. It always gave a single 'tink' sound about 8 or 9 seconds before it was about to ring. So whenever you heard it, you knew the ring was coming. Now this 'tink' had never really played a part in any of the games before but on this occasion it did...

So there I was, charging down the left-hand side, all poised to shoot when I heard it. 'Tink.' I glanced at the timer.

"Time!" shouted Dale.

"No it isn't!" I said, "It hasn't gone off yet."

"Nope, not yet," said Laurence who was acting referee. "There's a few seconds left."

I looked at Dale, he looked at me and we both _knew_ this was it! *The last kick of the match!* The world Cup would be decided by this one kick and I was going to take it. I took a deep breath, bent low over the table, set my hand and flicking finger behind my No. 11, my captain, *El Capitán*. If any player was going to win the match for me it would be him. Glory would soon be mine. I was going to score and win *The World Cup*!

In my mind I could hear the cheers. I was finally going to win the match and be crowned champion. Oh, the *adulation*. *I* would be the *World Champion*. Oh, the fame, the glory, the women!! Well, ok, maybe that was pushing it a bit far... but I was going to win. *I* was going to Mount Olympus and walk with gods. I could hear the fanfares and the angels singing...

More importantly, I could rub his bloody nose in it for a change! Oh, how I was going to strut into work on Monday morning, the rightful heir ascending his throne having crushed all before him. Finally I would be the one to gloat over Dale and say, "Thorners... Get 'em aht!" and he'd be the one who would have to dish his fags out. T-Dubs and the others would laugh and be ribbing him all day instead of me. Oh, how I was going to enjoy Monday.

I took careful aim, pulled back my finger then flicked...

What a shot! WHAT – A – SHOT!! What a beautiful, majestic – worthy of winning a *World Cup Final* – shot! *El Capitán* had struck the ball perfectly. It flew straight and true and with speed and accuracy, and it was rising...

Hallelujah! And just like every other game between Dale and me _this_ was going to be close... and the ball... it was still rising... I could hear the angels singing... What a shot... praise the lord... it's beaten the 'keeper... Glory would soon be mine... up and up it went... speeding towards Dale's goal... Hallelujah! I was delirious... Finally! The _real_ champ has arrived. Finally, at last... Victory!

I was in heaven...

Chapter 18.
I'm a Guy, Uruguay.

Later on that summer, I actually spent quite a bit of time with Dale. Sedge was bogged down with his girlfriend and both Dale and I were single at this point. Helen eventually got fed up with me going out with Dale and Paul or spending too much time playing Subbuteo and not spending enough time with her. 'Enough time' meant being round at her house every evening and basically spending every spare waking moment with her. This became so painfully tiring for both of us that we amicably decided to split.

This meant that I was single and free to come and go as I pleased and often went out with Dale. It turned out that we actually had an awful lot in common which was hardly surprising, considering we shared the same birthday.

It was great to have someone with whom you could go drinking with and have a laugh and a good time. And Dale used to do both. Jo summed him up best "Drink a lot, bonk a lot, brag about it later! That's Dale." She said. And she was right. He did. Incidentally, Jo turned out to be Janice's younger *sister*! It was her - not T-Dubs - who'd let on to Janice about Sedge and the lilac jumper. It also explained why she used to take Sherlock's typing down to the typing pool, so she could be the spy in the camp and update her sister on all the gossip.

So Dale and I would often go out pubbing and clubbing which generally involved drinking lots of beer and chatting-up women. Something else Dale was far better than me at! But it was all good, harmless fun and we enjoyed each others' company while it lasted.

The very last time I played Subbuteo against Dale was one Bank Holiday weekend in August when I went out for an all-day drinking binge with him at his club. Finally, I was being allowed into the 'inner-sanctum' of the 'Bexley-Heath Working Man's club' and Dale suggested a match.

I immediately accepted the challenge and we went to a corner of the club. There was an old games table with a block of chipboard leaning against the wall. Dale told me to lay it on the table while he went to the bar, returning with more beer, the Subbuteo pitch, his "Boyzees", a ball, some goalposts, an egg timer, and Steve's Uruguay. Obviously, as I had been unprepared for the match I didn't have my beloved Chile on hand so I had to use them.

The setup was basic to say the least with a pitch that was very flat, very hard and very bare – exactly like Chubby's. No wonder he was able to play so well on it! Only I had been spoilt by having a billiard table to lay my pitch on giving it the effect of a rich, well-fed pitch. Not like Dale's, which incidentally had beer stains, minor cigarette burns and fag ash on it as well.

So there we were, beer and fags in hand, in an old man's working club, no-one paying us the slightest mind at what we were doing and we kicked-off.

By half-time, the score was One – One. I had taken an early lead, only to get pegged back by a determined Dale as the familiar cry of "Boyzees!" broke through the boozy, smokey air!  Occasionally, someone would pass by the table, stop and watch for a few minutes and then saunter off to the toilets. Again I realised, this was why Dale was used to having a bit of an audience, he had one every time he played Steve in the club.

In the second half, Dale took the lead at Two – One with a few minutes to go on the clock and he celebrated with his traditional jig around the table and chanting "Boyzees!! Boyzees!! Boyzees!!"

However, his victory celebrations were a little premature, as I managed to get him on the back foot, and in the final moments managed to score an equaliser! Two – Two.

Finally, when the match ended we just hugged each other having fought yet another, great match to a draw.

Chapter 19.
A tie for the last time.

The last time I saw Dale it was in the autumn of 1982. I had left the company where we worked and had gone to America with an old school-friend for a six-month tour.

When I came back, I met up with Dale and Sedge who suggested a night out at a nightclub somewhere in Croydon for a few beers and a general catch-up together. When we got to the door of the nightclub the doormen turned us away as we weren't wearing ties. Dale made the suggestion that as I lived closest we could nip back to my house and get some, which we did.

Dale of course, chose my favourite tie which was a thin grey material type of tie which was in fashion at the time and Sedge and I grabbed a couple of others. Suitably attired, off we went to the nightclub.

The next morning I woke with a sore head and two ties. Mine and the one Sedge had been wearing but not Dale's. Then I vaguely remembered Dale saying that he'd spilt beer on it and he would get it dry-cleaned and bring it back to me...

Weeks and weeks passed and I never saw or heard from Dale at all. I would ring him but all he would say was "Yeah, yeah, I'll drop it round" or "I'll post it..."

But he never did.

Then one day, probably a full six or seven months later I was working in East Croydon just around the corner from the train station. I'd left work for the evening and was standing by my motor bike putting on my water-proofs and crash helmet when who should come strolling around the corner but Dale. He had just finished work himself and was walking towards me on his way to the station. He had a dark grey suit on... and my tie!

After a brief exchange of pleasantries and "How are you doing...?" I asked him for my tie.

"Oh, I'll er..." he'd forgotten he was wearing it "I'll er... get it cleaned and send it back to you..." he said.

"No. You won't" I said flatly. "You didn't last time and you won't this time. I'll take it now please!"

Dale slumped. He shook his head and gave that exasperated sigh that people do when they have to do something reluctantly, and he was certainly reluctant to hand it back to me. He slowly removed it from around his neck and with a pissed-off look handed it back to me. I put the tie in my pocket, chatted for a few more minutes, got on my bike and rode off.

That was the last time I ever saw him.

Goodbye !

Chapter 20.
For flicks sake!

"But what about that goal...?" I hear you ask. "That goal you scored when you won the World Cup? When the angels were singing and you beat Dale and you were being carried off to Mount Olympus. You never did quite finish the story..."

Really? You ask me this now? Why can't we finish it there? It's a perfect ending to my story... Ohhh alright then, if you insist. Where was I? Oh Yes, my game timer, it had just 'tinked' to alert us to the last few seconds of the match and I was poised, ready to shoot. My Captain, my faithful, ever dependable, 'El Capitán' was about to take the shot. Dale's eyes were filled with dread. We both *knew* this was it! The very last shot of the *World Cup Final*!

I took a deep breath to compose myself, bent down, set my hand on the table and then flicked. *El Capitán* sped towards the ball and caught it perfectly. It was a b-e-a-u-tiful shot! A powerful, manly, worthy-of-winning-a-world-cup-final-shot that whizzed towards Dale's goal like no other shot. This was going to rip the back of the net off the goal! Time for me seemed to slow right down as I could see everything so clearly. The ball was struck firm and hard and fast and was rising towards the goal. Dale moved his 'keeper but he was beaten all-ends-up. He was flapping and floundering at thin air at the near post but he was just too slow and too low to have stopped it. This was going in. It was heading for the top corner of the goal!

This shot was MAJESTIC! It just FLEW! It was *the most perfect shot* I'd ever made...!

The ball however, was not. That ball, that bloody ball. Again! It was <u>still</u> just a shade too light, and just a shade too small, and just a shade no sodding good to man nor beast - except Dale of course. The trajectory of the ball meant that it rose, and rose, and rose, until... it spanked hard into the crossbar and sailed high into the air over Dale's right shoulder and off into oblivion. And with it, went my World Cup dreams...

Bollocks!

I could have cried.

I'd bloody-well missed!!

Dale bent down and picked the ball up. He had a huge grin on his face. That HUGE, smug-bastard, punch-able grin that he always had when he was winning, and this time he *knew* he'd won. By the time he'd placed it back on the pitch for the goal kick, the tinny 'BRRRRINGGG!' of my clock sounded and ended the match once and for all. Dale was champion again.

I hadn't beaten him but also I hadn't *been* beaten by him – or anyone else for that matter, yet there it was. Once again he topped the table on goal difference, but unlike the last time there would be no replay.

I hadn't scored the winning goal so I didn't get the glory, or the fanfares, the plaudits, the fame, the fortune, the women, the bragging rights. Nothing! And neither was I crowned world champion. Not then, not ever.

Would I never beat Dale?

For flicks sake!

Dale was champion and I was not.

It was over.

Game 6.

Result: Chile 0 – 0 Peru

The 2nd World Cup 1981
Standings after 6th Game

Teams	PLD	W	D	L	G/F	G/A	Diff	PTS
Peru	3	2	1	0	7	0	7	5
Chile	3	2	1	0	6	1	5	5
England	3	1	0	2	4	7	-3	2
Belgium	3	0	0	3	0	9	-9	0

Chapter 21
'Boyzees!'

As I sit and write these words in 2021, I still can't believe all that happened almost forty years ago. Yet I can still remember it as though it were only last summer. I remember the excitement and fun we had. The highs, the lows, the agony, the ecstasy and the pain of being *just-oh-so-so close*... and generally, just the fun of playing Subbuteo again.

We were young men playing with toys from our childhood and we were enjoying every moment of it. I didn't realise it then but it was actually quite a special time, the friendships that we had, the rivalry and the camaraderie.

What memories...

Sadly, nowadays it is very rare for people to play table-top or board games, preferring instead to play computer games or games projected onto their television. It is such a shame as games like Subbuteo are so tactile and engaging that people miss-out on the social interaction that makes them such fun.

However, having said that, the computer age has actually helped to keep games like this alive. For example; on a well-know online auction website you can buy just about anything you could ever want to buy. There is always someone out there in cyberspace willing to buy or sell – for the right price – anything your heart desires, including Subbuteo.

In fact, towards the mid-late nineteen eighties, Subbuteo had practically died out. The teams were made of cheap, inferior plastic. The paint jobs were very poor. The players were all of a *light-weight* variety which meant that they played completely differently. Subbuteo was on its knees! It had been bought out by the games giant *Hasbro* from Peter Adolf who invented the whole thing but in my humble opinion, it just wasn't the same. By reducing the amount of plastic used to manufacture the teams, the players produced were thin, flimsy, and generally of inferior quality. They just didn't play the same way.

The internet however, gave access to the many, many fans of Subbuteo (sad men like me of a certain age it has to be said but...) it had a following. And the online auction websites were certainly taking advantage of this revival. Go on to one at any given time of the day and you will see literally thousands of Subbuteo items being advertised for sale every single day. It's so huge now that there are imitation companies such as *Santiago* and *Zeugo* selling very similar versions of the Subbuteo brand.

And you can buy anything, any team and any accessory. There are floodlights, scoreboards, trainers, substitutes, managers, trophies, fence-surrounds, pitches, even whole stadiums with running tracks around the pitch on them, everything. And of course, teams. Lots of teams. Teams you've never even heard of teams. You could buy the whole of the premiership, championship, first and second divisions. You could buy the top European teams. You could get obscure Australian, Canadian, American and South American teams, even second division Portuguese teams! You name them and now, you can get them. Or if you can't, then someone will paint them for you. You could even have your old school team colours painted for you. Yes, somehow, somewhere, someone is still manufacturing little plastic men to fit onto curved and weighted bases and selling them on, probably making a nice little living out of it too.

And as for me? Well, back then I thought I had quite a nice collection of Subbuteo. It was certainly the largest of anyone I ever knew. I had seventeen teams. Twenty if you counted the three Rugby teams I had. I thought that was a pretty large collection. But since then, I've discovered these online websites and now my collection is just over a hundred teams. I have every team I could have ever wished for. Some I bought just because they *looked* good but never knew who they were. Over twenty-something of them are South American, Caribbean or African teams... all very different looking and all very colourful. However, Chile is STILL my No.1 favourite.

It's funny. I have Sweden, I have Belgium and I have West Germany and Uruguay. I have Haiti, Spain, France, Zaire, Mexico, El Salvador and all manner of different teams. I even have a '*Roy of the Rovers*' Melchester Rovers team. But the one team I do not own is Peru. I just cannot bring myself to buy them. If you go online right now and typed in a search for '*Subbuteo Peru*' you will see a list of at least half-a-dozen to a dozen versions of Peru. Light-weight, heavyweight, red base, white inner or white base, red inner. There are loads of them.

But I will never buy them.

What would be the point? It wouldn't be *them*. It wouldn't be the "Boyzees!" and they wouldn't be the same *invincible* team that Dale owned that broke my heart. It would just be a pale imitation. There would be no point.

But every now and then, as I'm collecting my teams I do occasionally sit and think about them, wondering if me and my Chile were ever destined to beat them. And sometimes I think of Dale and wonder if he still has them, most probably not. He probably never even thinks about them, or our rivalry...

The "Boyzees!" most likely, are lost for all time, only to exist immortalised in my memory... and now, hopefully, forever in yours.

Boyzees!

The End.

That damned ball!

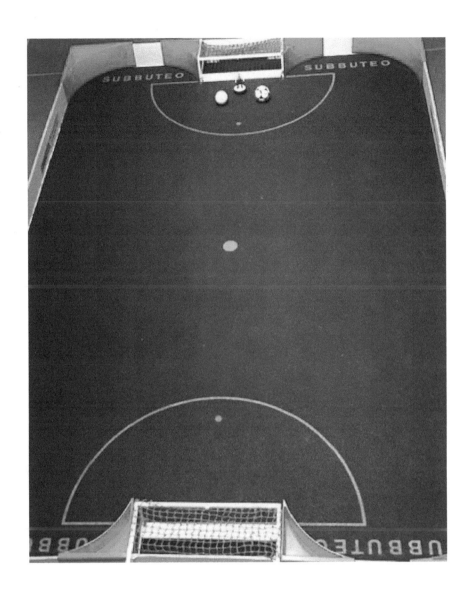

Subbuteo Five-A-Side Pitch

Ball-raising chute

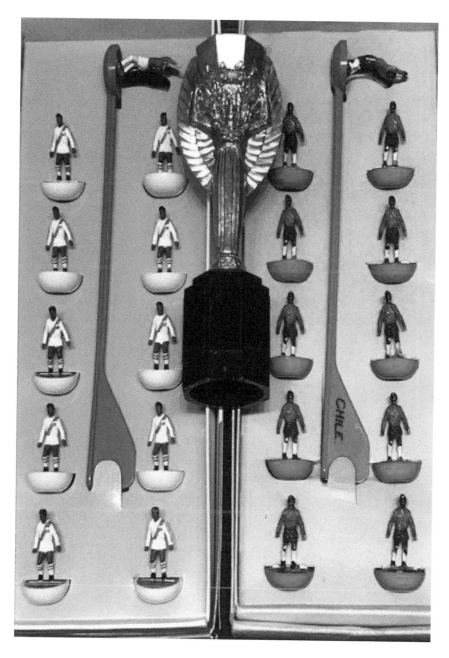

The Antagonists

List of matches between Dale and myself.

		At Chubby's House	
		Game 1	**Score**
		Peru	2
		Brazil	**0**

		Infamous Two-Legged Match				
Game 2	**Score**	**Game 3**	**Score**	**Score**	**Away Goals Count Double**	**Aggr.**
Peru	3	Peru	0	3	Peru	6
Chile	**2**	**Chile**	**1**	**3**	**Chile**	**4**

		World Cup Group Match	
		Game 4	**Score**
		Peru	3
		Holland	**3**

		World Cup Final	
		Game 5	**Score**
		Peru	2
		Holland	**1**

		World Cup Final	
		Game 6	**Score**
		Peru	0
		Chile	0

		Bexley W/man's Club	
		Game 7	**Score**
		Peru	2
		Uruguay	**2**

Tale of the Tape
Standings after 7* Games

(*Includes the 2 legged match as two games. 2 points per win, 1 point for a draw, nil for a loss)

Teams	PLD	W	D	L	G/F	G/A	Diff	PTS
Dale	7	3	3	1	12	9	7	9
Ashley	7	1	3	3	9	12	-3	5

Acknowledgements

To my beloved wife, Lillian. For her belief, love, patience, encouragement and unwavering support during the writing of this book. May you rest in peace my darling.

To my dear friends Suzi for proof-reading and helping me get this published and to Blondine and Rocky for keeping me inspired.

To my brothers Laurence and Terry. Thank you for teaching the eight-year old me, and for playing it with me. And thank you for the hours of practice you both gave me whilst growing-up.

To my mum and dad for buying me this amazing, wonderful game. Thank you!

To all my old work colleagues who added to the background tapestry for my tale.

Thank you to Paul (Sedge) for being such a good mate.

And finally, thank you to Dale for being impossible to beat! I could not have written this without you.

For Flicks Sake!

Milton Keynes UK
Ingram Content Group UK Ltd.
UKHW050637241023
431225UK00010B/69